IAN CHRISTIAN

Van-Life 101

The Essential Guide to your Life on the Road

Copyright © 2024 by Ian Christian

All rights reserved. No part of this publication may be reproduced, stored or transmitted in any form or by any means, electronic, mechanical, photocopying, recording, scanning, or otherwise without written permission from the publisher. It is illegal to copy this book, post it to a website, or distribute it by any other means without permission.

Ian Christian asserts the moral right to be identified as the author of this work.

Ian Christian has no responsibility for the persistence or accuracy of URLs for external or third-party Internet Websites referred to in this publication and does not guarantee that any content on such Websites is, or will remain, accurate or appropriate.

Designations used by companies to distinguish their products are often claimed as trademarks. All brand names and product names used in this book and on its cover are trade names, service marks, trademarks and registered trademarks of their respective owners. The publishers and the book are not associated with any product or vendor mentioned in this book. None of the companies referenced within the book have endorsed the book.

First edition

This book was professionally typeset on Reedsy.
Find out more at reedsy.com

Contents

1	Introduction	1
2	Choosing the Right Van for You	3
3	Self Sufficiency, The Off-Grid Dream	26
4	Comfort vs. Practicality	59
5	Home Comforts	104
6	Cooking on the Road	142
7	Planning Your First Adventure	184
8	Money-Saving Hacks	222
9	Conclusion	229
10	References	231

1

Introduction

Welcome to Van-life 101: Essential Hacks to Your Life on the Road! Whether you're just starting to dream about life on the road or you've already purchased your van and are itching to hit the highway, this guide is your perfect co-pilot. It's designed to give you practical, no-nonsense advice to make your van life journey as smooth, fun, and cost-effective as possible.

Life on the road is a unique adventure. It's freedom at its finest—waking up to new horizons, chasing sunsets, and living on your terms. But it's also about learning how to adapt, plan, and make the most of limited space, time, and resources. For first-timers, it can feel overwhelming to know where to begin: How do you choose the right van? What do you really need to go off-grid? How do you stretch every dollar while still making it a trip to remember?

That's where this book comes in. It's packed with tried-and-true hacks, clever shortcuts, and expert insights to help you hit the road with confidence. Whether you're flying solo, adventuring with a partner, or setting off with the whole family, you'll find guidance tailored to your journey. Each chapter is focused on a specific aspect of van life, from building out your dream vehicle to planning your first adventure, saving money, and staying comfortable along the way.

But this isn't just a how-to manual; it's also about mindset. Van life isn't about perfection. It's about creativity, resourcefulness, and embracing the unexpected. You'll learn how to balance practicality with adventure, find joy in the simple moments, and create a lifestyle that feels uniquely yours.

So, buckle up and get ready. This isn't just a guide to van life—it's the start of your next great adventure. Let's hit the road!

2

Choosing the Right Van for You

If van life is the heart of your new adventure, then your van is the soul. It's your transportation, your home, your safe haven, and possibly the most important decision you'll make as you start this journey. Choosing the right van isn't just about finding something that fits your budget; it's about picking a vehicle that fits you. Your lifestyle, your travel goals, and even your personality will all play a role in this decision. Let's break it down into the key factors you need to consider.

1. Size Matters (But Bigger Isn't Always Better)

When it comes to van life, the size of your vehicle is more than just a number—it defines your lifestyle on the road. From compact minivans to full-size bus conversions, your choice of vehicle size will impact everything from fuel costs to parking ease and even your comfort during a rainy week spent indoors. Let's explore the pros and cons of different van sizes to help you find the one that fits your needs, personality, and travel plans.

Compact Minivans: The Bare-Bones Adventure Mobile

Minivans like the Honda Odyssey, Toyota Sienna, or Dodge Grand Caravan are often
overlooked in the van life world, but they pack surprising potential.

Pros:
Exceptional fuel efficiency compared to larger vans, making them a budget-friendly
choice for long trips.

Easy to manoeuvre and park, even in busy cities or narrow mountain roads.

Perfect for solo travellers or minimalist couples who prioritise simplicity over space.

Cons:
Limited living space—forget about standing up or fitting a full kitchen.

Customisation options are minimal due to their small size, though clever storage
hacks can make a big difference.

Ideal for short-term trips or adventurers who prefer spending most of their time
outdoors.

Medium Vans: The Goldilocks Option

Medium-sized vans, like the Mercedes-Benz Metris, Ford Transit Connect, or Ram
ProMaster City, strike a balance between compact efficiency and functional space.

Pros:
Offers more space for sleeping, cooking, and storage while still being

relatively easy to
  drive and park.
Good for solo travellers, couples, or even a small pet.
Can be fitted with basic van life essentials like a bed platform, small kitchenette, and
  portable power.

Cons:

Less room for long-term storage or bulky gear, making it tricky for extended
  adventures or cold-weather travel when extra clothing is needed.
Not tall enough for most people to stand inside, which can limit comfort during bad
  weather.

Full-Size Vans: The Classic Van life Choice

Models like the Mercedes Sprinter, Ford Transit, and Ram ProMaster dominate the van
  life scene for a reason—they're versatile, spacious, and customizable.

Pros:

High roofs allow you to stand up and move around, which is a game-changer for full
  time van life.
Enough room to install luxuries like a full bed, kitchenette, and even a small bathroom
  setup.
Suitable for couples or small families, especially if you're hitting the road for months
  at a time.

Cons:

Lower fuel efficiency, especially with heavier builds.
More expensive upfront, especially for newer models or professional

conversions.

Can be harder to park in cities or navigate through narrow or rough terrain.

Bus Conversions: The Mansion on Wheels

If space is your ultimate priority, a school bus (or "skoolie") conversion or shuttle bus

could be the answer. These vehicles offer unparalleled room for creativity and comfort.

Pros:

Huge interior space, perfect for families or those who want full amenities, like

separate bedrooms, large kitchens, and full bathrooms.

Solid platforms for long-term living, with enough storage for everything you own.

Tons of charm and creativity—many skoolie conversions feel like tiny houses on

wheels.

Cons:

Poor fuel efficiency, making long trips costly.

Difficult to drive and park, requiring careful planning for routes and stops.

Hefty maintenance costs, especially for older buses.

Choosing Your Size: The Sweet Spot

Your van size depends on how you plan to use it. Weekend warriors might find a minivan all they need, while full-time adventurers will appreciate the space and amenities of a full-size van or bus. Remember, bigger isn't always better. Smaller vehicles mean more flexibility, less cost, and fewer headaches—but larger vehicles provide unmatched comfort and convenience for long-term travel.

Before you decide, think about your priorities: Where will you spend most of your time? How often will you travel? Do you need extra room for family or hobbies? Answering these questions will steer you toward the van that feels just right.

2. Age and Condition: Old Soul or New Ride?

One of the first big decisions when choosing your van is whether to go for a brand-new ride or a pre-loved vehicle. Both options have their merits, but they also come with unique challenges. Let's dig into the pros and cons of each, along with some real-world examples of what you might encounter when dealing with an older van.

New Vans: Fresh Off the Lot

There's a lot to love about buying a new van. It's shiny, clean, and packed with the
 latest features. But is it the right choice for van life?
Pros:
Reliability: A new van is less likely to break down, which means fewer unexpected
 repair bills and less time spent at the mechanic's shop.
Warranty Protection: Most new vans come with manufacturer warranties, giving you
 peace of mind for the first few years.
Fuel Efficiency: Modern vehicles are often more fuel-efficient, saving you money over
 the long haul.

Tech and Safety Features: From advanced navigation systems to collision-avoidance
tech, newer vans are packed with features that can make life on the road easier and
safer.

Cons:

High Initial Cost: New vans come with a hefty price tag, which can be a barrier for
budget-conscious travellers.

Rapid Depreciation: A new vehicle loses value the moment you drive it off the lot,
which might not be ideal if you decide van life isn't for you.

Less Customization Freedom: Some new vans come fully fitted, which might limit
your ability to personalise the build to your exact needs.

Popular Choices:
The Ford Transit and Mercedes Sprinter are go-to options for new van buyers, known
for their reliability and ample space.

Used Vans: Budget-Friendly with a Side of Quirk

For many first-time van lifers, a used van is the perfect starting point. These vehicles
are more affordable and often come with unique character. However, buying used
requires careful consideration.

Pros:

Lower Cost: Used vans are significantly cheaper than new ones, leaving more room in
your budget for customizations or travel expenses.

Customization Potential: With a lower initial investment, you can spend more on

creating your dream layout.

Diverse Options: From vintage VW buses to reliable Toyota HiAces, the used market

offers something for every style and budget.

Cons:

Potential Repairs: Older vans often come with a history of wear and tear. Be prepared

for maintenance issues, such as:

Rust: A common problem in older vehicles, especially those from humid or coastal

areas. Rust around wheel wells, undercarriages, or door frames can be costly to fix.

Engine Troubles: High-mileage engines may need expensive repairs like timing belt

replacements or gasket fixes.

Transmission Issues: Older vans with automatic transmissions are especially prone to

slipping gears or complete failure.

Outdated Systems: From lack of air conditioning to unreliable heating, older vans may

lack the comforts of modern vehicles.

Unknown History: Unless you're buying from a trusted seller, you may not know how

well the van was maintained or whether it was in accidents.

Popular Choices:

The Dodge Ram Van (for classic charm), Toyota HiAce (for legendary reliability), and

Ford E-Series (for its durability and abundant spare parts).

Real-World Example: New vs. Used in Action

The New Van Buyer: Sarah, a solo traveler, chose a brand-new Mercedes Sprinter. She loved the modern amenities, but the $60,000 price tag stretched her budget. While she enjoyed reliable travel and sleek features, she realized she couldn't afford the build-out she wanted until much later.

The Used Van Buyer: Jake and Emily bought a 15-year-old Dodge Ram Van for $8,000. They invested another $2,000 to replace the tires and fix some rust issues but had enough left over to create a fully customized interior. While they dealt with minor engine hiccups along the way, the savings made it all worth it.

So, What's the Right Choice?

The best choice depends on your budget, priorities, and willingness to get your hands dirty. If you value peace of mind and can afford it, a new van offers reliability and convenience. On the other hand, if you're up for the occasional repair and want to save money for travel or customizations, a used van might be your best bet.

Before you decide, always inspect the van thoroughly—or hire a mechanic to do it for you. Whether you choose new or used, taking the time to evaluate its condition will save you headaches and money down the road.

3. Budgeting: What's the True Cost?

Buying a van isn't just about the sticker price—it's the starting point of a bigger investment. From insurance and registration to maintenance and customizations, there are plenty of hidden costs that can catch first-time van lifers by surprise. Let's break down the true costs of owning a van and give you real-world examples to help you plan your budget wisely.

Initial Purchase Cost: The Starting Point

Your van's price tag is the first (and often the biggest) expense. This varies wildly
based on the van's size, age, and condition.

Budget-Friendly Options (< $10,000):

Older models like a Dodge Ram Van or a Ford Econoline.

Often requires immediate repairs (e.g., tires, brakes, or minor engine fixes).

Example: A 2002 Ford Econoline might cost $6,000, but you'll likely spend $1,500
replacing rusted parts and another $800 on tires.

Mid-Range ($10,000–$30,000):

Newer used models like a Ford Transit or Ram ProMaster with moderate mileage.

A balance between upfront cost and reliability.

Example: A 2015 Ford Transit with 80,000 miles might cost $22,000 and need only
minor updates, like new wipers or an oil change.

High-End ($30,000+):
Premium vans like a Mercedes Sprinter or fully converted ready-to-go options.
Perfect for buyers who value convenience and modern amenities.
Example: A 2021 Mercedes Sprinter with a prebuilt conversion could set you back
$80,000 but comes road-ready with solar panels, a kitchenette, and a bed.

Registration, Insurance, and Taxes
Once you've purchased the van, there are legal and administrative costs to consider.
Registration Fees: These vary by state or country and are often based on the weight
and value of the vehicle.
Example: Registering a Ford Transit in California might cost $150–$300 annually.
Insurance: Expect higher rates if your van is registered as an RV or if it has significant
modifications.
Example: Insuring a basic Ford Econoline might cost $80/month, while a fully
converted Mercedes Sprinter could be $200/month or more.
Taxes: Sales tax on a new van can add thousands.
Example: In a state with 8% sales tax, a $50,000 van will add $4,000 to your bill.

Repairs and Maintenance: Budget for the Unexpected
Every van, new or old, will need maintenance. It's smart to set aside an emergency
fund for surprise repairs.

Typical Maintenance Costs:

- Oil changes: $50–$150, depending on the van's size and type.
- Brake pad replacement: $200–$400 per axle.
- Tire replacement: $600–$1,200 for a full set of all-terrain tires.

Unexpected Repairs for Older Vans:

- Transmission repair: $2,000–$5,000.
- Replacing a timing belt: $500–$1,500.
- Fixing rust damage: $500–$3,000, depending on severity.

Real-World Example:

Mark bought a 2008 Dodge Sprinter for $15,000. Within six months, he spent $2,800
fixing the transmission and another $1,200 on new tires. While he loved his van, the
unplanned repairs stretched his budget.

Conversion and Build-Out Costs

Building out your van is where things can get as cheap—or as extravagant—as you
want.

DIY Builds:

Basic Setup: A mattress, portable stove, and basic storage might cost $500–$1,000.

Intermediate Setup: Adding insulation, a solar panel, and a sink could run $3,000 -
$5,000.

Example: Julia spent $4,000 outfitting her Ram ProMaster with a bed frame, cabinets, and a solar-powered fridge.

Professional Conversions:
Custom builds from companies like Off-Grid Adventure Vans or Outside Van start at
$20,000 and can exceed $100,000 for luxury models.
Example: A professional build on a Mercedes Sprinter, complete with a full
kitchenette, shower, and lithium battery setup, could total $120,000.

Fuel Costs: Your Lifeline on the Road
Fuel expenses depend on your van's size and how far you travel. Larger vans typically
have lower fuel efficiency.
Compact Vans: 20–25 mpg. Example: A Toyota Sienna might cost $75 for a 500-mile
trip.
Full-Size Vans: 14–18 mpg. Example: A Ford Transit might cost $125 for the same trip.
Bus Conversions: 8–12 mpg. Example: A skoolie might burn through $200–$250 on
that 500-mile stretch.

Real-World Budget Breakdown
Here's a snapshot of what you might expect to spend in your first year of van life:
Budget Van (Used Ford Econoline):

- Purchase: $8,000
- Registration and insurance: $1,000

- Repairs: $2,000
- DIY build-out: $2,500
- Fuel (12,000 miles/year): $2,500
- **Total**: ~$16,000

Mid-Range Van (Used Ford Transit):

- Purchase: $25,000
- Registration and insurance: $1,500
- Minor repairs: $800
- DIY build-out: $4,000
- Fuel (12,000 miles/year): $3,000
- **Total**: ~$34,300

High-End Van (Mercedes Sprinter with Professional Build):

- Purchase: $80,000
- Registration and insurance: $3,000
- Professional build: Included
- Fuel (12,000 miles/year): $3,500
- **Total**: ~$86,500

Plan Ahead for Peace of Mind

The true cost of van life goes beyond the initial purchase. By planning for these additional expenses, you'll avoid unwelcome surprises and set yourself up for a smoother ride. Whether you're on a tight budget or ready to splurge, understanding the financial commitment upfront is the key to making van life sustainable and enjoyable.

4. Ready-Built vs. Self-Build

One of the biggest decisions when diving into van life is deciding how to set up your van: Should you go for a ready-built van that's road-ready from day one, or take the DIY route with a self-build? Each option has its strengths and challenges, and the right choice depends on your budget, skills, and how much time you're willing to invest. Let's explore the pros and cons of both approaches and look at real-world examples to help you decide.

Ready-Built Vans: Hit the Road Immediately
Ready-built vans, whether purchased from a professional conversion company or a
previous owner, come fully outfitted and ready to roll.
Pros:
Time-Saving: Skip the months (or years) of planning and building. With a ready-built
van, you can hit the road as soon as you sign the papers.
Professional Quality: Conversions from companies like Outside Van or Winnebago are
designed with efficiency and durability in mind. They often include high-quality
materials, tested layouts, and advanced systems like lithium batteries and efficient
plumbing.
Turnkey Convenience: Everything you need—like a bed, kitchen, and storage—is
already installed. Perfect for those who value ease over customization.
Cons:
High Initial Cost: Professional conversions are expensive, often

doubling or tripling
the cost of the van itself.

Limited Customization: You're locked into the builder's design, which might not fully
meet your needs or preferences.

Repairs Can Be Tricky: If something breaks, proprietary parts or designs can make DIY
repairs difficult and expensive.

Real-World Example:
Lucy and Dan bought a 2020 Mercedes Sprinter professionally converted by Off-Grid
Adventure Vans for $85,000. They loved the sleek layout and high-quality appliances
but quickly found that the built-in kitchen didn't suit their cooking style. They had to
spend an additional $1,500 to reconfigure the countertop and storage space.

Self-Build Vans: A Labor of Love
Building your own van gives you complete control over the design and features, but
it's not for the faint of heart.

Pros:
Cost-Effective: A DIY build can save you thousands compared to a professional
conversion.

Fully Customized: Tailor the layout to your exact needs, whether it's a workspace,
extra storage for outdoor gear, or a pet-friendly setup.

Learn Valuable Skills: From carpentry to electrical wiring, you'll gain

hands-on
knowledge that makes future repairs and upgrades easier.
Cons:
Time-Consuming: Building a van can take months, especially if you're learning as you
go.
Skill and Tools Required: Without prior experience, the learning curve can be steep,
and mistakes might cost you both time and money.
Potential for Imperfections: A DIY build might not match the polish or durability of a
professional job.

Real-World Example:
Tom bought a used Ford Transit for $20,000 and spent six months building it out
himself with a $5,000 budget. While he loved customizing the layout to include a bike
storage rack and outdoor shower, he underestimated the complexity of wiring his
solar panels. After several frustrating attempts, he had to hire an electrician for $600
to fix the system.

Hybrid Option: The Best of Both Worlds
For those who want a balance between convenience and personalization, consider
starting with a partially built van.

Partially Converted Vans: Some sellers offer vans with insulation, flooring, and basic setups already installed, leaving room for you to add your own touches.

Customized Professional Builds: Some companies allow you to work with their designers to create a layout tailored to your needs.

Real-World Example:
  Sophie and Mark bought a partially converted Ram ProMaster for $40,000. It came
  with insulation, a bed platform, and plumbing for a sink. They spent another $3,000
  adding a solar setup and customized storage, getting the best of both worlds: a solid
  starting point and the freedom to personalize.

Making the Choice
  Ask yourself:

- **How much time and effort are you willing to invest?** If you're short on time or lack the skills, a ready-built van might be the better option.
- **What's your budget?** A self-build is often cheaper, but keep in mind that unexpected costs can add up.
- **How important is customization?** If you have specific needs or a unique vision, a self-build gives you full creative control.

Whatever you choose, remember: It's not just about the van—it's about the journey. Whether you buy ready-made or build it yourself, the right van is the one that takes you to the adventures you've been dreaming of.

5. Test Drives and Gut Checks

Before you commit to your future home on wheels, it's crucial to take it for a test drive—both literally and figuratively. A test drive gives you a chance to evaluate how the van feels on the road and how well it fits your lifestyle. Whether you're buying new or used, this step can save you from costly regrets later. Here's how to make the most of this critical stage and ensure you're making the right decision.

During the Test Drive: Feel the Road
Getting behind the wheel is your first opportunity to experience the van's handling,
   comfort, and quirks. Here's what to focus on:

Steering and Handling:
   Does the van feel stable on the road?
   Is the steering responsive, or does it feel loose?
   Test it on different terrains: highways, city streets, and rougher roads if possible.

Acceleration and Braking:
   Does the van accelerate smoothly, or does it lag?
   Are the brakes responsive without making noises like squealing or grinding?

Noise Levels:
   Listen for unusual sounds like clunking, whining, or rattling, which could indicate
      underlying issues.
   Evaluate general road noise. Is it tolerable for long drives, or will you need to invest in

insulation?

Comfort:
Check the seating position and overall visibility. Can you comfortably see and operate
everything?
Ensure you have enough legroom and space to drive comfortably on long journeys.

Turning Radius and Parking:
Test its turning radius to ensure it can navigate tight spaces or winding roads.
Try parking it to see if the size is manageable for you.

Inspect the Van Inside and Out
Even if the test drive feels great, don't skip a detailed inspection. Look for signs of
wear and tear that could indicate future problems:

Exterior Check:

- **Rust**: Focus on wheel wells, undercarriages, door frames, and roof seams. Surface rust might be manageable, but structural rust is a red flag.
- **Body Damage**: Look for dents or poorly done repairs, which could signal past accidents.
- **Tires**: Check tread depth and wear patterns. Uneven wear might mean alignment issues.

Interior Inspection:

- **Leaks**: Check for water stains on ceilings or walls, especially near windows and doors. Leaks can lead to mold or structural damage.
- **Condition of Seats and Flooring**: Worn-out upholstery or cracked flooring can indicate how hard the van's been used.
- **Odors**: Strange smells might suggest leaks, mold, or other hidden issues.

Under the Hood:

- **Fluids**: Inspect oil, coolant, and transmission fluid levels and colors.
- **Battery**: Check for corrosion and ensure the battery is in good condition.
- **Belts and Hoses**: Look for cracks or signs of wear that could lead to breakdowns.

Ask Questions (and Get Answers)

Whether you're buying from a dealership or a private seller, don't be afraid to ask
detailed questions. The answers can reveal a lot about the van's history and potential
future.

For Used Vans:
"Has the van been in any accidents?"
"What repairs or maintenance have been done recently?"
"Why are you selling the van?"

For New Vans or Conversions:
"What's covered under the warranty?"

"Are there any add-ons or upgrades available?"
"Can I customize certain features?"

Gut Checks: Living With Your Choice

Beyond the technical details, take a moment to imagine your daily life in the van. This
 is where your gut feelings come into play:

Space and Layout:

Walk around inside. Does the space feel cramped or just right for your needs?

Picture your day-to-day life—cooking, sleeping, relaxing. Can you see it working?

Practicality:

Think about where you'll park. Is the van too large for city streets or too small for your
 gear?

Consider storage. Will it accommodate all your essentials comfortably?

Emotional Connection:

Does this van feel like *the one*? Sometimes, you just know. If it doesn't excite you, keep
 looking.

Pro Tips for Test Drives

Bring a Mechanic:

If you're not confident in your ability to assess the van's mechanical condition, bring a
 trusted mechanic to inspect it. Spending $100–$200 on a pre-

purchase inspection can
   save you thousands down the road.
Compare Multiple Vans:
Don't buy the first van you test drive. Try out several options to get a sense of what
   feels best.
Take Your Time:
A rushed decision is often a regrettable one. Don't let a pushy seller or an enticing deal
   pressure you.
Test Everything:
Check all the van's systems, including lights, wipers, air conditioning, heating, and
   any additional features like awnings or power outlets.

Real-World Example: A Cautionary Tale

Matt fell in love with a used Dodge Ram Van that seemed perfect for his budget and needs. During the test drive, he noticed a slight shimmy at high speeds but ignored it. After purchasing the van, he discovered the issue was due to a damaged drive shaft, which cost $1,800 to replace. The lesson? Trust your instincts, and don't ignore potential problems, no matter how minor they seem.

The Final Decision

A test drive is about more than mechanics—it's about making sure the van feels like home. By paying attention to the details, asking the right questions, and trusting your gut, you'll set yourself up for a choice that brings you joy every mile of the journey. Remember, the perfect van isn't just a vehicle; it's your ticket to freedom and adventure. Choose wisely!

3

Self Sufficiency, The Off-Grid Dream

For many van lifers, the allure of off-grid living is a major draw. It's not just about saving money on utility bills—it's the freedom to park in the middle of nowhere, away from hookups and noisy campgrounds, while still having all the essentials for daily life. Achieving true self-sufficiency in your van means designing a setup that supports your energy, water, and waste needs without relying on outside sources. Let's explore how to create an off-grid lifestyle that keeps you comfortable and independent.

1. Powering Your Van: Off-Grid Energy Solutions

Power is the lifeblood of your off-grid van life. Whether you need to charge your devices, run lights, power a refrigerator, or even use small appliances, a reliable and sustainable energy setup is essential. Off-grid power systems may seem complex, but with the right planning, you can create a setup that keeps your van fully powered, even in remote locations. Let's dive deeper into the details of building an off-grid energy system that works for you.

Solar Power: The Off-Grid Gold Standard

Solar power is the most popular and reliable way to power a van off-grid. It provides
free, renewable energy that's perfect for long-term travel without depending on
hookups or noisy generators.

Solar Panels:

Types:

Rigid Panels: Durable and efficient, ideal for mounting on the roof.

Flexible Panels: Lightweight and easier to install on curved surfaces but slightly less
efficient.

Portable Panels: Freestanding panels you can set up at camp to maximize sun
exposure.

How Many Watts Do You Need?

Start by calculating your energy needs. For example:

Running a small fridge: ~40–70 watts/hour

Charging a laptop: ~50 watts/hour

LED lights: ~10 watts/hour

A 200W–400W solar setup works well for most van lifers. Larger systems (600W or
more) are better for those running high-demand appliances like induction cooktops or
electric heaters.

Example Setup:

300W solar panels with a 30A charge controller can generate around 1,200 watt-hours
per day in good sunlight—enough to power a fridge, lights, and small

electronics.

Charge Controller:

A charge controller regulates the energy flowing from your panels to your batteries,

preventing overcharging. Look for MPPT (Maximum Power Point Tracking)

controllers, which are more efficient than PWM (Pulse Width Modulation) controllers.

Battery Bank:

Lithium-Ion Batteries: Lightweight, long-lasting, and efficient, but they're

expensive.

AGM Batteries: Affordable and maintenance-free but heavier and with a shorter

lifespan.

Capacity: Aim for at least 100Ah of storage for basic setups, or 200Ah+ for heavier

usage.

Inverter:

Converts DC power from your batteries into AC power for appliances.

Types:

Pure Sine Wave: Ideal for sensitive electronics and appliances.

Modified Sine Wave: Cheaper but less reliable for advanced devices.

Other Power Sources for Off-Grid Living

While solar is the mainstay of most van setups, it's wise to have backup options for

cloudy days or heavy usage periods.

Portable Generators:

Pros: Reliable backup power and capable of running high-demand appliances.

Cons: Noisy, require fuel, and not eco-friendly.

Popular Models: Honda EU2200i (quiet and efficient) or Jackery Explorer 2000 (a

solar-compatible generator with battery storage).

Shore Power:

If you occasionally stay at RV parks or campgrounds with electrical hookups, shore

power can recharge your batteries.

Requires an inverter/charger that can convert external AC power into battery charge.

Alternator Charging:

Your van's alternator can charge your battery bank while driving. This is a great

supplementary power source, especially for short-term off-grid setups.

Power Management: Make Every Watt Count

A well-designed power system is only half the equation. Managing your energy use

effectively is just as important to ensure you don't run out of power when you're off

grid.

Energy-Efficient Appliances:

Use 12V appliances whenever possible, as they draw directly from your batteries

without needing an inverter.

Choose an energy-efficient fridge, like the Dometic CFX series, which

consumes as
   little as 1Ah/hour.

LED Lighting:
   LED lights use a fraction of the energy of traditional bulbs. Install dimmable lights to
   control usage further.

Turn Off Devices When Not in Use:
   Phantom loads from devices on standby can drain your batteries over time. Use power
   strips with switches to easily cut off power to unused items.

Real-World Example: A Solar-Powered Success
   Laura and Mike, full-time van lifers, wanted to stay off-grid for weeks at a time while
   working remotely. They invested in a 400W solar setup with two 100Ah lithium
   batteries and a 2,000W pure sine wave inverter. This system powers:

- A 12V fridge running 24/7.
- Two laptops for remote work.
- LED lights and a MaxxAir fan.

Cost Breakdown:

- Solar panels, charge controller, and mounting kit: $1,200
- Lithium batteries: $2,000
- Inverter and wiring: $500 **Total**: $3,700

Their system allows them to stay off-grid for up to two weeks, even during cloudy weather, while comfortably running all their appliances.

Planning Your System

When designing your off-grid power system, start with these steps:

Calculate Your Energy Needs: Make a list of all the devices you'll use, how long they'll run, and their power requirements (in watts or amps).

Choose Your Power Sources: Decide on solar as your primary source, with backups like alternator charging or a portable generator.

Invest in Quality Components: Spend a little extra on reliable equipment to avoid headaches later.

With the right setup, your van can generate and store enough power to keep you comfortable, connected, and independent no matter where the road takes you. Solar panels might be the star of off-grid living, but smart planning and efficient energy use are what make the dream a reality.

2. Water Systems: Stay Hydrated and Clean

Water is essential for off-grid living. Whether you're drinking it, cooking with it, or using it to stay clean, having a reliable water system is crucial for maintaining comfort and self-sufficiency on the road. A well-thought-out water setup includes storage, filtration, and waste management, giving you the ability to go days—or even weeks— without needing to refill. Here's how to plan and build a water system that keeps you hydrated, clean, and off-grid ready.

Water Storage: How Much Do You Need?

The size of your water storage depends on how many people are traveling, how long you plan to stay off-grid, and what you'll use the water for. Here's what to consider:

Daily Water Use Estimates:

- Drinking: 1–2 gallons per person.
- Cooking: 1–2 gallons per day.
- Cleaning (dishes and hygiene): 2–4 gallons per day.
- **Total**: For two people, plan on at least 5–8 gallons per day.

Storage Options:

Portable Water Containers:

- Flexible and affordable. Great for those with limited space or a smaller van.
- Example: The Reliance Aqua-Tainer holds 7 gallons and is easy to refill.

Built-In Tanks:

- Installed under seats, inside cabinets, or beneath the van. These are ideal for larger setups or those who want to minimize the hassle of frequent refills.
- Common sizes range from 10 to 50 gallons.

Tips for Maximizing Space:

- Use stackable or collapsible water containers to save space when empty.
- Install a tank underneath your van to free up interior room.

Water Filtration: Clean and Safe

When you're off-grid, you might not always have access to treated water. A filtration
system ensures you can safely drink from natural sources like rivers, lakes, or
questionable campground taps.

Types of Filtration Systems:

- **Portable Filters**:
- Great for emergencies or small-scale filtration.
- Example: LifeStraw Go Bottle filters up to 1,000 gallons.
- **Inline Filters**:
- Installed directly in your water system, providing constant filtration for all your water use.
- Example: Camco TastePURE RV Water Filter.
- **Gravity Systems**:
- Use gravity to filter large volumes of water at once.
- Example: Platypus GravityWorks is popular for van lifers.
- **Purifiers**:
- Devices like SteriPENs use UV light to kill bacteria, viruses, and protozoa in untreated water.
- **When to Filter**: Always filter water from natural sources or public taps with uncertain quality. Even treated water can benefit from filtration to improve taste and remove potential contaminants.

Plumbing: Getting Water Where You Need It

A functional water system needs more than just storage and filtration—it requires
efficient plumbing to deliver water where you need it.

Pump Options:

- **Manual Pumps**: Simple and reliable, these require no electricity. Perfect for budget builds.
- **Electric Pumps**: Provides on-demand water flow, like a traditional tap. Requires power but is much more convenient.

Example: Shurflo 12V water pump is a van life favorite.

- **Faucets and Showers**: Install a small faucet over your sink for washing dishes or filling bottles. Outdoor showers can be plumbed into your system using a retractable hose. Some even use portable solar showers for hot water on a budget.

Grey water Management: Handling Wastewater

Grey water—used water from sinks and showers—needs proper handling to avoid
environmental damage or health hazards.

Grey water Tanks:

Collect grey water in a dedicated tank or jug, usually placed beneath your sink or
mounted under the van.

Typical sizes range from 5 to 10 gallons.

Disposal Tips:

Always empty your grey water at designated dump stations or into sewer systems.

Use biodegradable soaps to minimize environmental impact if disposing of grey water
in nature (only where permitted).

Hot Water Options: Luxuries Off-Grid
If you're planning on hot showers or heated water for washing, you'll need a heating
solution.

Solar Showers:
Affordable and easy to use. Fill the bag, leave it in the sun, and enjoy warm water.
Example: Nemo Helio Pressure Shower.

Propane Water Heaters:
Compact heaters provide on-demand hot water. Ideal for larger setups or families.
Example: Eccotemp L5 portable tankless water heater.

Electric Heaters:
Requires significant power, so only viable with a robust solar system.

Real-World Example: A Well-Designed Water Setup
Katie and Rob, a couple living in their converted Ford Transit, prioritized a robust
water system for extended off-grid stays. Here's their setup:

- **40-Gallon Built-In Freshwater Tank**: Supplies two weeks of water for drinking, cooking, and cleaning.
- **Camco Inline Filter**: Filters all incoming water during refills to ensure safe drinking water.
- **Shurflo 12V Pump**: Delivers pressurized water to their sink and outdoor shower.
- **5-Gallon Grey water Tank**: Collected waste is easily emptied at

dump stations.
- **Solar Shower**: Used for warm outdoor showers when camped in sunny locations.

Cost Breakdown:

- Freshwater tank: $150
- Inline filter: $20
- Water pump and plumbing: $120
- Grey water tank: $40
- Solar shower: $35**Total**: ~$365

Their system has allowed them to camp off-grid for up to 10 days at a time while staying hydrated and clean, proving that a well-planned water setup doesn't have to break the bank.

With a thoughtfully designed water system, you can stay hydrated, cook delicious meals, and enjoy refreshing showers no matter how far you roam. By combining sufficient storage, effective filtration, and proper greywater management, your van will be fully equipped for off-grid adventures.

3. Cooking Off-Grid: Portable and Efficient Solutions

Good food is a cornerstone of van life, and cooking off-grid doesn't mean sacrificing delicious meals. With the right tools and techniques, you can create a mobile kitchen that's compact, efficient, and versatile enough to handle everything from a quick snack to a gourmet dinner. Let's explore how to set up your cooking system and keep your culinary adventures alive on the road.

Choosing the Right Stove: The Heart of Your Mobile Kitchen

Your stove is the most important component of your off-grid cooking setup. Here are
the main types of stoves and their pros and cons:

Propane Stoves

Why Choose Propane? Reliable, widely available fuel, and excellent heat control make
propane stoves the go-to choice for van lifers.

Popular Models: Coleman Triton and Camp Chef Everest are highly recommended for
their durability and efficiency.

Pros:
Easy to use with adjustable flame control for precise cooking.
Works in all weather conditions, including wind and cold.

Cons:
Requires a safe place to store propane tanks.
Not eco-friendly, as it relies on fossil fuels.

Butane Stoves

Why Choose Butane? Ideal for occasional cooking or smaller setups, butane stoves are
lightweight and portable.

Popular Models: Iwatani 35FW is a compact and reliable choice.

Pros:
Compact and easy to store.
Affordable and beginner-friendly.

Cons:
Struggles in very cold weather as butane doesn't vaporize well below freezing.

Electric Induction Cooktops

Why Choose Induction? Perfect for those with a robust solar and battery system,
induction cooktops offer clean, efficient, and flameless cooking.

Popular Models: Duxtop 1800W Portable Induction Cooktop is energy-efficient and
compact.

Pros:
No open flame, reducing fire risk inside the van.
Highly energy-efficient, cooking faster than gas stoves.

Cons:
Requires significant battery capacity and inverter power.
Can't be used off-grid without a strong solar system.

Refrigeration: Keeping Food Fresh

Having a way to store fresh ingredients is a game-changer for long-term off-grid
living.

12V Compressor Fridges

The most popular choice for van lifers due to their energy efficiency and compact size.

Popular Models: Dometic CFX series and ARB Element are highly rated.

Pros:
Uses minimal power, around 1–2 amps per hour.
Maintains consistent temperatures for reliable refrigeration or freezing.

Cons:
High upfront cost ($500–$1,500).

Coolers

A budget-friendly alternative, coolers rely on ice or ice packs to keep food cold.

Popular Models: YETI and RTIC coolers are known for their long ice retention.

Pros:

Affordable and easy to use.

No power required.

Cons:

Requires frequent ice replenishment, which can be inconvenient.

Food Storage Solutions: Maximize Space and Minimize Waste

When living in a van, efficient food storage is essential to avoid clutter and waste.

Non-Perishables:

Stock up on staples like rice, pasta, oats, canned goods, and dehydrated foods. These

take up minimal space and last a long time.

Store them in stackable, airtight containers to protect against pests and spills.

Fresh Ingredients:

Choose fruits and vegetables with a long shelf life, such as apples, carrots, and

potatoes.

Use mesh bags to improve airflow and reduce spoilage.

Spices and Condiments:

A compact spice rack or magnetic tins can help keep your seasonings organized.

Transfer condiments into small, travel-sized containers to save space.

Cookware and Tools: Keep It Simple and Functional

You don't need a full kitchen's worth of tools to cook off-grid. Focus on multipurpose
items that save space and weight.

Essential Cookware:

A medium-sized nonstick frying pan and a small pot with a lid are versatile enough for
most meals.

Consider nesting cookware sets to save space.

Cutting Tools:

A good-quality chef's knife and a small cutting board are must-haves.

Collapsible cutting boards double as strainers for pasta or rinsing vegetables.

Other Must-Haves:

A silicone spatula, wooden spoon, and tongs.

A French press or AeroPress for coffee lovers.

A collapsible sink for washing up.

Maximizing Efficiency While Cooking Off-Grid

Meal Prepping:

Plan meals that use minimal ingredients and cookware. One-pot meals like stews,
curries, or stir-fries are ideal.

Pre-chop ingredients and store them in reusable containers for quick assembly.

Energy and Water Conservation:

Use lids on pots and pans to cook food faster and save fuel.

Reuse boiled water for washing dishes or soaking dirty pans.

Cooking Outdoors:

A portable camping table and folding chairs can transform any campsite into a functional outdoor kitchen.

Cooking outside also reduces heat buildup inside your van.

Real-World Example: The Perfect Off-Grid Kitchen

Sam and Alex, a couple traveling in their converted Sprinter van, have created a compact yet functional off-grid kitchen. Their setup includes:

- **Cooking**: A Coleman Triton propane stove and a Duxtop induction cooktop for backup.
- **Refrigeration**: A Dometic CFX3 45L fridge, which runs on their 200Ah lithium battery system.
- **Storage**: Stackable containers for dry goods, a hanging fruit hammock, and magnetic spice tins.
- **Tools**: A nesting cookware set, silicone utensils, and a collapsible sink.

Their efficient system allows them to cook everything from quick breakfasts to multi-course dinners, all while staying off-grid for up to two weeks.

With the right tools and strategies, cooking off-grid can be just as enjoyable and satisfying as cooking at home. By focusing on efficiency, versatility, and a bit of creativity, you'll be able to whip up delicious meals no matter where your van takes you.

4. Heating and Cooling: Comfort in Every Climate

Van life is as much about adapting to the elements as it is about embracing freedom. Whether you're braving snowy mountain passes or sweltering desert heat, staying comfortable in your van requires planning and the right tools. A well-designed heating and cooling system will not only improve your daily life but also extend the seasons and locations you can comfortably explore. Here's how to equip your van for comfort in every climate.

Heating: Staying Warm When Temperatures Drop

When winter weather hits or you're camping at higher altitudes, a reliable heating

system can make all the difference.

1. Diesel and Propane Heaters: Compact and Reliable
Diesel Heaters:

Powered by your van's fuel supply (or a separate diesel tank), diesel heaters are

efficient and compact.
Popular Models: Webasto Air Top 2000 or Eberspacher D2.
Pros:

Extremely fuel-efficient, using only a small amount of diesel per hour.
Heats the van quickly and evenly.
Doesn't require a separate fuel source if your van runs on diesel.
Cons:
Higher upfront cost (~$800–$1,500, including installation).
Requires proper venting to prevent carbon monoxide buildup.
Propane Heaters:
Popular Models: Mr. Heater Buddy or Propex HS2000.

Pros:
Propane is widely available and affordable.
Heats small spaces quickly.
Cons:
Requires careful monitoring and ventilation to avoid oxygen depletion or
condensation.
Less efficient for long-term or high-altitude use.

2. Electric Heaters: Clean and Quiet
Electric space heaters are great if you have a robust solar setup or access to shore
power.
Pros:
No fuel required, making them eco-friendly.
No need for venting or monitoring.
Cons:
High power demand (requires a large battery bank and inverter).
Not practical for off-grid use without a significant solar system.

3. Insulation: Your First Line of Defense
Proper insulation minimizes heat loss and reduces the energy required to keep your
van warm.
Recommended Materials:
Thinsulate: Lightweight, mold-resistant, and easy to install.
Foam Board: Rigid and effective for insulating walls, floors, and ceilings.
Reflectix: Great for windows and small spaces but less effective for large surfaces.

Cooling: Beating the Heat in Warm Climates

When summer heat rolls in, keeping your van cool is just as important as heating it in
winter.

1. Ventilation Fans: A Must-Have for Every Van

Popular Models: MaxxAir Fan Deluxe or Fantastic Fan.

How They Work: These 12V fans circulate air throughout the van, pulling hot air out
and drawing cooler air in.

Pros:

Low power consumption (uses about 2–3 amps per hour).

Can be run while parked or driving.

Some models include rain sensors and reversible airflow for added versatility.

Cons:

Requires roof installation.

Can't cool the air, only circulate it.

2. Portable Fans: Budget-Friendly and Effective

Compact, battery-operated fans are great for localized cooling.

Example: OPolar or Geek Aire rechargeable fans.

Pros:

Affordable and easy to move around.

Doesn't require installation or a permanent power source.

Cons:

Less effective for cooling large spaces.

3. Portable Air Conditioners: Powerful but Energy-Hungry

For extreme heat, portable AC units provide true cooling but come with high power

demands.
Popular Models: Zero Breeze Mark 2 or EcoFlow Wave.
Pros:
Cools the air effectively, making it ideal for hot climates.
Compact and portable.
Cons:
Expensive (units can cost $800–$1,200).
Requires significant battery capacity or shore power to run.

4. Passive Cooling Strategies: Low-Cost and Sustainable

Window Covers: Use reflective covers like Reflectix to block out sunlight and keep the
   interior cool.

Shade Parking: Always park in the shade when possible, and consider using an awning
   for additional cover.

Cross-Ventilation: Open windows on opposite sides of the van to create airflow.

Humidity Control: The Overlooked Comfort Factor

Whether you're heating or cooling, controlling humidity is essential for comfort and
   preventing issues like condensation or mold.

Dehumidifiers: Compact 12V models like Eva-Dry are perfect for reducing humidity in
   small spaces.

Moisture Absorbers: Budget-friendly options like DampRid can help control
   condensation without using power.

Real-World Example: A Van Built for All Seasons

Emma and Ryan, full-time van lifers, wanted to ensure they could travel comfortably
year-round. Here's how they equipped their Sprinter van:

- **Heating**: Installed a Webasto diesel heater that uses less than 0.1 gallons of fuel per hour.
- **Cooling**: A MaxxAir fan and Reflectix window covers keep the van cool in summer.
- **Insulation**: Thinsulate insulation throughout the van reduces energy needs for both heating and cooling.
- **Humidity Control**: They use an Eva-Dry dehumidifier during winter to prevent condensation buildup.

Cost Breakdown:

- Diesel heater: $1,200 (including installation).
- MaxxAir fan: $300.
- Insulation: $600.
- Dehumidifier: $80.**Total**: ~$2,180

Their setup allows them to comfortably explore snowy mountains in the winter and sunny deserts in the summer.

Planning Your Comfort System
   Evaluate Your Climate Needs: Do you spend more time in cold or hot regions?
   Prioritize heating or cooling based on your travel plans.
   Invest in Dual-Use Systems: Insulation and ventilation improve comfort in all
      climates, making them essential for every van.
   Plan for Efficiency: Choose systems that balance performance with

energy
consumption to maximize off-grid time.

With the right heating and cooling solutions, you'll enjoy the freedom to explore any environment without compromising comfort. Whether it's a chilly winter morning or a scorching summer afternoon, your van can become a cozy sanctuary in every season.

5. Waste Management: Staying Clean and Green

Proper waste management is a key part of off-grid van life. When you're parked far from facilities, you need a reliable system to handle everything from trash and recycling to human waste. A well-thought-out waste management plan not only keeps your van clean and odor-free but also minimizes your environmental impact. Let's dive into the options and strategies for staying clean and green on the road.

Managing Human Waste: Choosing the Right Toilet

Having a toilet in your van is a game-changer for convenience and off-grid
independence. Here are the most popular options:

1. Portable Toilets

How They Work: Portable toilets consist of a top compartment with a seat and flush
mechanism, and a bottom tank for waste collection.

Popular Models: Thetford Porta Potti or Camco Standard Portable Toilet.

Pros:
Affordable and compact.

Easy to empty at dump stations or public restrooms.
Cons:
Limited capacity, requiring frequent emptying.
Can develop odors if not maintained properly.

2. Composting Toilets

How They Work: These toilets separate liquid and solid waste, using materials like
sawdust or coconut coir to compost the solids.
Popular Models: Nature's Head and Separett Tiny.
Pros:
Eco-friendly and odor-free if maintained correctly.
Requires less frequent emptying than portable toilets.
Cons:
High upfront cost ($800–$1,200).
Bulkier and more complex to install.

3. Bag-Based Systems (Emergency or Minimalist Options)

How They Work: Waste is collected in biodegradable bags and sealed for proper
disposal.
Popular Systems: Luggable Loo or WAG Bags.
Pros:
Extremely lightweight and portable.
No installation required.
Cons:
Not ideal for long-term or frequent use.
Disposal can be inconvenient in remote areas.

Trash Management: Keeping Your Van Tidy

Trash can quickly pile up in a small space, so having a system in place is essential.

Storage Solutions:
Use a small, lidded trash can or hanging bag to keep waste contained.
For long trips, consider separating trash into recyclables, compostables, and landfill
waste using stackable bins.

Minimizing Waste:
Avoid single-use items and opt for reusable alternatives like cloth napkins, stainless
steel straws, and silicone food storage bags.
Buy in bulk to reduce packaging waste.

Disposal Tips:
Plan ahead by identifying trash and recycling facilities along your route.
Always pack out your trash if no proper disposal site is available.

Recycling: Reducing Your Environmental Impact

Recycling on the road can be challenging but not impossible.

Collection Tips:
Rinse and crush recyclables like cans and bottles to save space.
Use collapsible bins or mesh bags to store recyclables separately.

Finding Facilities:
Use apps like iRecycle or Earth911 to locate nearby recycling centers.
Many grocery stores and gas stations have bottle or can drop-off bins.

Grey water Management: Handling Wastewater

Grey water from sinks and showers needs to be managed responsibly to avoid
polluting the environment.

Storage Options:

Install a dedicated grey water tank under your van, with a capacity of 5–10 gallons.

For smaller setups, use a portable jug that can be manually emptied.

Disposal Guidelines:

Only empty grey water at designated dump stations, RV parks, or sewer connections.

Use biodegradable soaps and cleaning products to minimize environmental impact if

grey water is released in nature (only where permitted).

Composting Organic Waste: A Green Solution

If you cook often in your van, composting food scraps can reduce trash volume and

minimize odors.

Portable Composting Solutions:

Use a compact compost bin with a lid to contain scraps until you can add them to a

larger compost system or dispose of them at a composting facility.

Quick Composting Tips:

Freeze scraps in a reusable bag to prevent odors until you can compost them.

Avoid composting meat, dairy, or oils, as these attract pests and take longer to break

down.

Odor Control: Keeping Your Van Fresh

A clean waste system is an odor free waste system. Here's how to keep your van

smelling fresh:

Human Waste:

For portable toilets, add deodorizing tablets or liquids to the waste tank.

Composting toilets benefit from proper aeration and frequent addition of dry
materials like sawdust.

Trash:
Empty trash and recycling regularly, especially if storing organic waste.
Use trash bags with odor blocking features.

Grey water:
Clean grey water tanks periodically with a mix of vinegar and water to prevent buildup.

Real-World Example: A Waste Management Setup That Works

Matt and Sarah, full-time van lifers, have a comprehensive waste management
system that allows them to stay off-grid for extended periods:

- **Toilet**: Nature's Head composting toilet for eco-friendly waste management and infrequent emptying.
- **Grey water**: A 7-gallon tank with a drain valve for easy emptying at dump stations.
- **Trash and Recycling**: A small lidded trash can and collapsible recycling bins stored under the sink.
- **Composting**: A countertop compost bin for food scraps, which they empty at community gardens or compost facilities.
- **Odor Control**: Regular use of enzyme-based cleaners for tanks and bins keeps their van smelling fresh.

Plan Ahead for a Cleaner Adventure

Managing waste is an unavoidable part of van life, but with the right

systems, it can be
 easy and eco-friendly. By prioritizing sustainability and planning for proper disposal,
 you'll enjoy a cleaner, greener van life experience while leaving a minimal
 environmental footprint. Whether you're camping deep in the woods or parked by the
 beach, these waste management strategies will keep you fresh, tidy, and ready for your
 next adventure.

6. Connectivity: Staying Connected Without Hookups

In an increasingly digital world, staying connected is often essential— even when you're off-grid. Whether you're working remotely, navigating unfamiliar areas, or just keeping in touch with friends and family, reliable connectivity can make van life more enjoyable and less stressful. While going completely off-grid has its charm, having a plan for staying connected ensures you have access to information, entertainment, and help when needed. Here's how to build a connectivity setup that works, no matter how far off the beaten path you go.

Cellular Service: The Backbone of Connectivity

Most van lifers rely on cellular networks for their internet and communication needs.

Here's how to maximize coverage and reliability:

Choose the Right Carrier:

Coverage varies widely between carriers. Research which provider offers the best service in the regions you plan to visit.

In the U.S., Verizon and AT&T tend to have the widest rural coverage, while T-Mobile

excels in urban areas.

Unlimited Data Plans:

Look for plans with truly unlimited data if you rely on your phone or hotspot for

internet. Some plans throttle speeds after a data cap, which can slow you down.

Popular Options: Visible (by Verizon) offers affordable unlimited plans, while AT&T

and T-Mobile have options tailored to RVers.

Boosting Cellular Signal: Staying Connected in Remote Areas

When you're far from cell towers, a weak signal can make communication impossible.

Signal-boosting tools can help:

Cellular Signal Boosters:

Devices like the **weBoost Drive Reach** or **HiBoost Travel** amplify weak signals,

improving call quality and internet speeds.

How They Work: The booster captures faint cellular signals with an external antenna,

amplifies them, and rebroadcasts them inside your van.

Pros:

Extends your usable range in remote areas.

Works with most carriers and devices.

Cons:

Cannot create a signal where none exists.

Directional Antennas:

Pairing a booster with a directional antenna can further improve signal strength.

These antennas require manual adjustment to point at the nearest cell tower but offer

better performance in extremely remote areas.

Mobile Hotspots: Your Personal Wi-Fi Hub

For those who need consistent internet for work or streaming, a mobile hotspot is a

game-changer.

What Is a Mobile Hotspot?

A device that connects to a cellular network and broadcasts a Wi-Fi signal for your

devices. Some smartphones can double as hotspots, but dedicated devices often

perform better.

Popular Hotspot Devices:

Netgear Nighthawk M1: Reliable, fast, and compatible with multiple carriers.

T-Mobile Inseego 5G MiFi M2000: Great for high-speed internet where 5G is

available.

Tips for Maximizing Your Hotspot:

Position it near a window or use an external antenna to improve reception.

Monitor your data usage to avoid overage charges or throttling.

Satellite Internet: Connectivity Anywhere

For van lifers venturing into extremely remote areas, satellite internet provides a

lifeline.

Starlink RV (Now Starlink Roam):
A game-changing option for high-speed internet virtually anywhere.
Pros:
Works in locations with no cellular coverage.
Provides speeds fast enough for video calls, streaming, and uploading large files.
Cons:
High upfront cost (~~$599 for hardware~~) and monthly fees (~~$135+~~).
Requires clear skies and open space to connect to satellites.
Traditional Satellite Services:
Services like HughesNet or Viasat are options, but they're slower and more expensive
than Starlink, with higher latency.

Offline Tools: When Connectivity Fails

Even with the best setup, there will be times when you're completely off-grid.

Planning for these moments ensures you can navigate and stay informed without
internet access.

Offline Maps:

Download maps from Google Maps or apps like Gaia GPS before heading out. Offline
maps provide detailed navigation even without a signal.

Apps for Offline Use:

iOverlander: Find campsites, water sources, and dump stations.

Park4Night: A go-to for van lifers in Europe.

AllTrails: Access hiking trails and reviews offline.

Emergency Communications:

Devices like the Garmin InReach or SPOT Satellite Messenger allow text messaging and GPS tracking via satellite, making them essential for safety in remote areas.

Powering Your Connectivity Setup

Your devices need power to stay connected, so make sure your van's power system can
support them:

Charging Devices:

Use 12V USB ports or a small inverter to charge phones, hotspots, and laptops.

Solar-powered battery packs provide a backup for charging small devices.

Energy Efficiency Tips:

Turn off Wi-Fi and cellular on devices not in use to conserve battery.

Use low-power modes on smartphones and hotspots to extend their runtime.

Real-World Example: A Reliable Connectivity Setup

Jess and Tom, full-time digital nomads, needed a connectivity solution that worked
for both remote work and travel. Here's their setup:

- **Carrier and Plan**: Verizon unlimited data with an AT&T backup SIM.
- **Signal Booster**: weBoost Drive Reach to improve coverage in rural areas.
- **Hotspot Device**: Netgear Nighthawk M1, providing stable internet for two laptops and a smart TV.
- **Satellite Internet**: Starlink Roam for remote locations where cellular coverage is unavailable.
- **Offline Tools**: Google Maps offline, Gaia GPS, and a Garmin

InReach for emergencies.

Cost Breakdown:

- Signal booster: $500
- Hotspot device: $300
- Starlink Roam hardware: $599
- Monthly data plans (combined): $200 **Total**: ~$1,600 upfront, $200/month ongoing.

Their setup allows them to work remotely, stream movies, and stay connected even in the most remote locations.

Planning for Connectivity Success

Assess Your Needs: Are you working remotely, or do you just need occasional
connectivity for navigation and updates? Tailor your setup accordingly.

Invest in Redundancy: A combination of cellular, satellite, and offline tools ensures
you'll always have a way to stay connected.

Optimize Your Budget: Start with essentials like a hotspot or signal booster, and
expand your setup as needed.

With the right connectivity tools, you can maintain the perfect balance of freedom and connection. Whether you're uploading work projects from a forest clearing or finding your way back to the main road, staying connected ensures your off-grid lifestyle is as smooth and stress-free as possible.

Real-World Example: Living Off-Grid Successfully

Anna and Jake converted a Ram ProMaster into a self-sufficient off-grid home. Their setup includes:

- A 400W solar panel system powering a 12V fridge, LED lights, and an induction cooktop.
- A 40-gallon fresh water tank with an inline filter and a 5-gallon greywater jug.
- A diesel heater for cold nights and a MaxxAir fan for ventilation.
- A composting toilet to avoid frequent waste disposal trips.

Their upfront investment in off-grid features totaled $8,000, but it allows them to camp in remote locations for up to two weeks at a time without resupplying.

The Off-Grid Dream, Made Real

Creating a self-sufficient van setup isn't just about gadgets and gear— it's about

designing a lifestyle that aligns with your values of freedom, sustainability, and

independence. By investing in the right systems, you'll gain the confidence to park

wherever the road (or trail) takes you, knowing that your van is equipped to keep you

comfortable, clean, and powered up for the adventure ahead.

4

Comfort vs. Practicality

Living in a van means embracing small spaces, but it doesn't mean sacrificing comfort. Striking the right balance between comfort and practicality is key to making your van a cozy, functional home on wheels. With smart design, creative storage solutions, and budget-friendly upgrades, you can maximize your available space without draining your bank account. Let's explore how to make your van as comfortable as possible while keeping it practical for life on the road.

1. Prioritize Multi-Functional Spaces

In a van, every inch of space needs to work double (or triple) duty. Multi-functional spaces are the cornerstone of both comfort and practicality, helping you make the most of limited square footage without feeling cramped. By designing areas that serve multiple purposes, you'll maximize efficiency while keeping your van cozy and functional. Here's how to prioritize multi-functional design in your van build.

1. Convertible Furniture: One Piece, Many Uses

Furniture that changes form to suit your needs is a game-changer in small spaces.

Convertible Beds:

Day-to-Night Transformation: A bed that converts into a sofa or dinette during the

day frees up valuable living space.

Popular Configurations:

Pull-Out Beds: A slide-out platform that turns a couch into a bed.

Folding Beds: Murphy-style or trifold beds that fold away when not in use.

Dinette-to-Bed Conversions:

Install a removable or collapsible table between two bench seats. Lower the table and

add cushions to create a sleeping area at night.

Example: Many DIY van lifers use this setup for two-person builds, as it offers a full

dining and sleeping area in one.

Flip-Up Countertops:

Extend your kitchen counter with a hinged countertop extension. This extra space can

double as a prep area, work desk, or dining surface.

2. Storage-Integrated Seating

Seating is essential, but it doesn't need to be a space hog. Adding storage under your

seats is an easy way to double their functionality.

Bench Seats with Storage:

Build bench seating with a hinged lid or pull-out drawers underneath. Use this space

to store bedding, shoes, or tools.

Example: A bench seat near the door can double as a place to remove

shoes while
  keeping clutter hidden.
Ottomans with Hidden Storage:
Compact ottomans are great for lounging and can store blankets, books, or electronics.

3. Folding and Collapsible Furniture

Folding or collapsible furniture lets you create functional spaces when you need them
  and clear them away when you don't.
Wall-Mounted Tables and Desks:
Attach a folding table or desk to the wall that can be stowed flat when not in use. Ideal
  for working or dining.
  Example: A small, drop-leaf desk can turn into a workspace or coffee table with a
  quick flip.
Folding Chairs:
Keep a set of compact, foldable chairs that can be used inside or outside. Look for
  lightweight aluminum or canvas options that are easy to store.
Collapsible Camping Tables:
Use a collapsible table that can serve as an extra dining or prep surface outdoors and
  packs away neatly inside the van.

4. Hidden and Slide-Out Features

Hidden or slide-out components maximize functionality without taking up visible
  space.
Slide-Out Kitchen Units:

Build a slide-out stove or sink that tucks away into a cabinet when not in use. This

saves counter space and keeps your van looking neat.

Pull-Out Pantry:

A narrow pull-out pantry unit can store dry goods, spices, and snacks in an otherwise

unused space, like next to the fridge or under the counter.

Hidden Desks or Workspaces:

Install a pull-out desk under your bed or in a cabinet. Combine it with a folding chair

for a complete workstation.

5. Versatile Outdoor Spaces

Don't forget to extend your living area outdoors, especially when the weather is nice.

Rear Slide-Out Storage:

Build a slide-out storage system in the rear of your van for easy access to gear, tools,

or even a pull-out table for outdoor cooking.

Awning Setups:

Install an awning to create a shaded outdoor living room. Combine it with collapsible

furniture for a comfortable seating area.

Rooftop Lounges:

Add a rooftop platform with foldable chairs or cushions to create an elevated lounge

space with a view.

Real-World Example: Multi-Functional Design in Action

Case Study: Emily and Jake's DIY Van Build

Emily and Jake, a couple traveling full-time in their self-built Ford

Transit, designed
their van with multi-functionality in mind:

- **Living Area**: A dinette with storage benches converts into a queen-size bed at night. The center table is removable, doubling as a laptop desk.
- **Kitchen**: A slide-out stove tucks under the counter, while a flip-up countertop creates additional prep space.
- **Outdoor Extension**: They added a rear slide-out storage drawer for camping gear, complete with a pull-out cutting board for outdoor meal prep.

Their setup allows them to maximize every square inch of their van while maintaining a clean and comfortable living space.

Tips for Designing Multi-Functional Spaces

Plan for Versatility: When building or buying furniture, ask yourself, "Can this do
more than one thing?" If not, rethink the design.

Test Layouts Before Committing: Use cardboard mock-ups or temporary furniture to
visualize how your space will flow before installing permanent fixtures.

Think Outside the Box: Look for inspiration in tiny homes or boat interiors, where
multi-functional designs are a necessity.

Prioritizing multi-functional spaces transforms your van into a versatile and efficient home, allowing you to live comfortably without feeling cramped. By combining creativity with smart design, you can make every part of your van work harder for you.

2. Maximize Comfort in Your Sleeping Area

Sleep is non-negotiable, especially when you're living on the road. A good night's rest keeps you energized for adventures and makes van life more enjoyable. Since your sleeping area is one of the largest and most important parts of your van, it's worth prioritizing both comfort and practicality. Here's how to maximize comfort in your sleeping area without sacrificing valuable space.

Choosing the Right Bed Setup
Your bed is the centerpiece of your sleeping area, and there are several configurations
to consider based on your van's size and layout.

- **Fixed Beds**:
- **Why Choose a Fixed Bed?**
- Ideal for full-time van lifers who want a ready-to-use bed at all times.
- Works well in larger vans like Sprinters, Transits, or ProMasters.
- **Design Tips**:
- Build the bed platform high enough to create ample storage underneath for bulky items like bikes, camping gear, or luggage.
- Use slatted platforms for ventilation to prevent moisture buildup under your mattress.
- **Convertible Beds**:
- **Why Choose a Convertible Bed?**
- Perfect for smaller vans where space is at a premium.
- Offers flexibility by transforming into a couch or dinette during the day.
- **Popular Options**:
- **Pull-Out Beds**: A couch that slides out into a bed.

COMFORT VS. PRACTICALITY

- **Dinette Conversion**: Benches with a table in between that lowers to create a sleeping platform.
- **Murphy Beds**:
  - **Why Choose a Murphy Bed?**
  - Provides a full-size bed that folds up against the wall when not in use.
  - Great for maximizing floor space while keeping a larger sleeping area.
- **Design Tips**:
  - Add storage pockets or shelves on the underside of the Murphy bed for extra functionality when it's folded up.

Selecting the Right Mattress

Your mattress plays a major role in sleep quality. Don't skimp here—invest in
something that offers proper support and comfort.

Types of Mattresses:

Memory Foam: Popular for van builds due to its ability to be cut to custom shapes and
sizes. Provides excellent comfort and pressure relief.

Latex Foam: A natural alternative that's breathable, durable, and hypoallergenic.

Folding or Roll-Up Mattresses: Ideal for convertible beds that need to store compactly
during the day.

Customizing for Your Van:

Measure your space carefully and trim your mattress to fit unusual dimensions.

Use a mattress cover or topper for added comfort and to protect against wear.

Bedding Essentials for Maximum Comfort

The right bedding makes all the difference in keeping you warm in the winter and cool

in the summer.

Blankets and Comforters:

Choose lightweight down or synthetic down comforters for optimal insulation that

packs small.

Use layers for flexibility—swap out heavy blankets for lighter ones in warmer weather.

Sheets and Covers:

Opt for moisture-wicking, quick-drying materials like bamboo or microfiber,

especially if you're in humid climates.

Use fitted sheets to keep everything in place, even on odd-sized mattresses.

Pillows:

Invest in compressible or inflatable pillows for easy storage.

For added support, choose memory foam travel pillows.

Optimizing the Sleeping Environment

Comfort isn't just about your bed—it's also about the surrounding space and

atmosphere.

Ventilation:

Install a roof vent fan (like MaxxAir or Fantastic Fan) near your sleeping area to

maintain airflow and reduce condensation.

Use vented windows or small portable fans to improve cross-ventilation.

Lighting:

Add soft, warm LED strip lights or dimmable puck lights around the bed for a cozy ambiance.

Include a reading light or clip-on lamp for nighttime use.

Temperature Control:

Insulate the walls around your sleeping area to maintain a comfortable temperature.

Use Reflectix or insulated window covers to block heat or cold.

A compact, energy-efficient heater or fan can keep the temperature just right.

Storage Solutions for Your Sleeping Area

Your bed doesn't just need to be comfortable—it also needs to be functional. Smart

storage solutions can help you maximize space.

Under-Bed Storage:

Use large plastic bins, drawers, or duffel bags to store clothing, shoes, and gear.

Install a sliding drawer system for easy access to items stored deep under the bed.

Overhead Storage:

Build cabinets above your bed for items like books, electronics, or personal essentials.

Use elastic nets or small shelves to keep frequently used items within arm's reach.

Side Pockets and Organizers:

Attach fabric or mesh organizers to the side of your bed frame for storing phones,

chargers, and water bottles.

Real-World Example: A Dreamy Sleeping Setup

Lily and Mark, a couple living in their converted Ram ProMaster, designed their
sleeping area to prioritize comfort and practicality:

- **Fixed Bed**: A high platform bed provides enough storage underneath for their camping gear and a folding bike.
- **Memory Foam Mattress**: Custom-cut to fit their van's dimensions, with a waterproof cover to protect against spills.
- **Bedding**: A lightweight down comforter and bamboo sheets keep them cozy in all seasons.
- **Lighting**: Warm LED strip lights under the cabinets provide soft, indirect lighting, while a clip-on reading light adds functionality.
- **Ventilation**: A MaxxAir fan above the bed ensures cool nights even in warmer climates.

Cost Breakdown:

- Bed frame materials: $250
- Memory foam mattress: $300
- Bedding and pillows: $100
- Ventilation fan: $300 **Total**: ~$950

Their setup offers hotel-level comfort in a van, proving you don't need to sacrifice quality sleep on the road.

Tips for Enhancing Sleep Quality in a Van
   Keep It Dark: Use blackout curtains or Reflectix window covers to block out light and
   ensure privacy.
   Stay Organized: Make your bed every morning and keep the sleeping area clutter-free

for a more relaxing space.

Prioritize Quiet: Park in quiet areas, use earplugs, or add soundproofing materials to
your van to reduce noise.

A comfortable sleeping area is the heart of a well-designed van. With the right setup, you'll look forward to restful nights that recharge you for the adventures ahead. By combining smart storage, cozy bedding, and thoughtful layouts, you can create a space that feels like a true sanctuary—no matter where you park.

3. Create an Efficient Kitchen

A well-organized and efficient kitchen is essential for van life. Whether you're whipping up quick meals or experimenting with gourmet dishes, having a functional kitchen setup can make your van feel like a true home. Designing your kitchen to maximize space, minimize waste, and accommodate off-grid living will ensure you can cook comfortably wherever the road takes you.

Choosing the Right Appliances

Compact and energy-efficient appliances are the backbone of an efficient van kitchen.

Stove Options:

Propane Stoves: A favorite among van lifers due to reliability and affordability. Choose
a dual-burner model like the Coleman Triton for versatility.

Butane Stoves: Compact and lightweight, ideal for smaller setups or occasional cooking.

Induction Cooktops: Great for those with robust solar and battery setups, offering

clean, flameless cooking.

Refrigeration:

12V Compressor Fridges: Energy-efficient models like the Dometic CFX series are

perfect for keeping food fresh without draining your battery.

Coolers: A budget-friendly option for short trips, though they require frequent ice

replenishment.

Tips:

Place your fridge or cooler in a ventilated area to prevent overheating.

Opt for models with dual-zone compartments for simultaneous refrigeration and

freezing.

Sink and Faucet:

Install a small stainless steel sink for washing dishes and prepping food.

Pair with a 12V electric pump or a manual foot pump for water flow, depending on your

power setup.

Maximizing Counter Space

Counter space is often limited in vans, so creative solutions are essential.

Foldable Counter Extensions:

Add a flip-up countertop on hinges that can be stowed when not in use.

Example: A flip-up cutting board near your sink can double as extra prep space.

Sliding or Pull-Out Counters:
Install pull-out surfaces under your main counter for additional workspace.
Use heavy-duty drawer slides to support heavier items like chopping boards or
portable stoves.
Dual-Purpose Surfaces:
Use sink covers or stove lids to create a flat surface when the appliances are not in use.

Smart Storage Solutions

Storage is critical to keeping your van kitchen organized and functional.
Cabinets and Drawers:
Opt for soft-close, locking mechanisms to prevent rattling and spillage during travel.
Install pull-out drawers with dividers to organize utensils, pots, and pantry items.
Overhead Storage:
Add cabinets above the kitchen counter for lightweight items like spices, dry goods, or
dishware.
Use elastic nets or bungee cords inside cabinets to secure contents.
Vertical Storage:
Magnetic knife strips or hooks can hold knives, spatulas, and other tools on the wall.
Add hanging baskets for fresh produce like fruit, garlic, or onions.
Hidden Storage:
Utilize under-seat compartments or toe-kick drawers for less frequently used items.
Store collapsible dish racks or folding bowls in tight spaces.

Efficient Food Preparation

Cooking in a small space requires thoughtful planning and preparation.

Prepping Tools:

Invest in multipurpose cookware, such as a skillet that doubles as a baking dish.

Use stackable or nesting pots and pans to save space.

A compact food processor or handheld blender can be a great addition for smoothies,

soups, or sauces.

Cutting and Chopping:

Use a lightweight, non-slip cutting board that fits your countertop dimensions.

Collapsible cutting boards with built-in strainers save both space and effort.

Quick Cleaning:

Keep a small, portable dish rack or drying mat near the sink.

Use biodegradable soap and a collapsible sink bucket for washing dishes outside when

off-grid.

Energy Efficiency in the Kitchen

Cooking in a van often relies on limited power, so minimizing energy use is critical.

Low-Energy Appliances:

Choose appliances designed for 12V systems or those with low wattage.

Use a pressure cooker to reduce cooking times and save fuel.

Use Lids on Pots and Pans:

Covering cookware traps heat, speeding up cooking and conserving energy.

COMFORT VS. PRACTICALITY

Batch Cooking:
Prepare meals in larger quantities and store leftovers for quick reheating later.

Waste Management in the Kitchen
Managing food waste and trash is essential for cleanliness and sustainability.

Trash and Recycling:
Use a small, lidded trash bin and separate recyclables into collapsible containers.
Empty trash frequently to avoid odors in a confined space.

Composting:
Keep a compact compost bin for food scraps, which can be emptied at community
   gardens or compost facilities.

Reusable Alternatives:
Swap single-use items for reusable options like silicone storage bags, beeswax wraps,
   and cloth towels.

Real-World Example: A Functional Van Kitchen Setup
Mike and Sarah, a couple living in their converted Mercedes Sprinter, designed a
highly efficient kitchen that meets all their cooking and storage needs:

- **Appliances**: A Dometic CFX3 fridge, a dual-burner propane stove, and a collapsible electric kettle.
- **Counter Space**: A flip-up countertop extension doubles their prep area.
- **Storage**: Pull-out pantry drawers for dry goods and overhead

cabinets for dishware. Magnetic strips and hooks keep utensils organized.
- **Cleaning**: A collapsible dish rack and portable sink bucket for easy dishwashing.
- **Power Management**: Solar panels power their 12V fridge, while propane handles most of their cooking needs.

Cost Breakdown:

- Fridge: $900
- Stove: $120
- Sink and plumbing: $200
- Countertops and cabinets: $600**Total**: ~$1,820

Their setup allows them to cook anything from simple breakfasts to elaborate dinners, all while staying off-grid for weeks at a time.

Tips for Designing Your Van Kitchen
  Plan Your Workflow: Arrange appliances and storage so everything you need is within
   arm's reach.
  Test Layouts: Before committing to a build, mock up your kitchen layout with
   cardboard or temporary furniture to ensure it feels functional.
  Start Simple: Begin with the basics and add extras as you discover your cooking habits
   on the road.

An efficient kitchen makes van life more enjoyable, whether you're cooking a quick meal after a hike or hosting a roadside dinner. By combining thoughtful design with versatile tools, you can create a kitchen that's functional, compact, and perfect for life on the road.

4. Make the Most of Seating and Living Areas

Your seating and living areas are the heart of your van—a place to relax, eat, work, and even entertain. In a small space, designing a multi-functional, comfortable living area is critical for creating a van that feels like home. By prioritizing versatile furniture, maximizing space, and adding personal touches, you can transform even the coziest of vans into an inviting and functional living room.

Optimize Seating for Comfort and Functionality
Your seating setup should be flexible enough to serve multiple purposes while
remaining comfortable for long periods.

- **Swivel Seats**:
- **Why They're Great**: Adding swivel bases to your van's front seats lets you repurpose them as part of your living area, saving space and improving functionality.
- **Installation Tips**:
- Ensure the seat can rotate without hitting adjacent surfaces or walls.
- Many aftermarket swivel bases are available for popular vans like Sprinters and Transits.
- **Bench Seating with Storage**:
- **Benefits**: Built-in benches double as storage compartments for items like blankets, tools, or outdoor gear.
- **Design Options**:
- Add cushions for comfort and create a cozy nook for relaxing or

dining.
- Build pull-out drawers under the bench for easy access to stored items.
- **Modular Seating**:
- Use stackable or modular cushions that can function as seats, footrests, or even a temporary bed for guests.
- Example: A cube ottoman with a hollow interior can provide extra seating, storage, and even a tabletop.

Create a Multi-Functional Living Area

In a van, your living space often serves as your dining room, workspace, and lounge.

Foldable or Removable Tables:

Wall-Mounted Tables: Attach a folding table to the wall that can be stowed when not

in use, freeing up floor space.

Removable Pedestal Tables: These tables can be easily set up between benches for

meals or work and removed when you need more open space.

Swing-Out Tables: Install a pivoting table arm that can swing into place when needed

and tuck away when not in use.

Convertible Living Space:

Install a dinette setup where bench seats surround a central table. By lowering the

table and adding cushions, you can quickly transform the area into a guest bed or

lounging platform.

Use collapsible furniture to create an adaptable space for activities like yoga, gaming, or hosting friends.

Design for Comfort and Ambiance
Small touches in your seating and living areas can greatly enhance comfort and
atmosphere.

Cushions and Upholstery:
Use high-density foam cushions for long-lasting comfort on bench seats.
Choose durable, easy-to-clean fabrics for upholstery, especially if you have pets or
kids.

Lighting:
Install dimmable LED lights or wall-mounted sconces for adjustable lighting.
Add string lights or battery-powered lanterns for a cozy, ambient glow.

Color and Texture:
Use throw blankets, decorative pillows, and rugs to add warmth and personality to
your living area.
Stick to a cohesive color scheme to make the space feel larger and more unified.

Add Entertainment and Connectivity Options
Make your living area a place where you can unwind and enjoy downtime.

Compact Entertainment Systems:
Mount a small TV or tablet holder for movie nights or streaming.
Use a portable Bluetooth speaker for music or podcasts.

Workspace Setup:

Install a fold-down desk or a pull-out tray for laptops or notebooks. Use a comfortable, ergonomic chair or add a cushion to your swivel seat for long work
sessions.

Outdoor Living Extensions
Expand your living space by taking the party outside.
Awning Setups:
Add a retractable awning to create a shaded outdoor area for lounging or dining.
Use weatherproof fabric for all-season protection.
Portable Furniture:
Keep folding chairs, stools, or a collapsible table in your storage area for outdoor use.
Look for lightweight, weather-resistant options that are easy to transport.
Outdoor Accessories:
String up solar-powered lights or lanterns to create a cozy atmosphere at night.
Keep an outdoor rug or mat handy to define your outdoor space and reduce dirt tracked
into the van.

Real-World Example: A Comfortable and Versatile Living Area
Emma and Lucas, full-time van lifers in a DIY-converted Ram ProMaster, designed
their living area for maximum comfort and flexibility:

- **Seating**: Swivel front seats combine with a bench seat to create a cozy lounge. The bench includes hidden storage for their shoes and winter gear.

- **Table**: A removable pedestal table serves as their dining area, work desk, and occasional coffee table.
- **Ambiance**: String lights along the ceiling and a patterned throw rug make the space feel warm and inviting.
- **Outdoor Extension**: A collapsible camping table and chairs stored under their bed allow them to set up a full dining area outside, complete with a roll-out awning.

Cost Breakdown:

- Swivel seat bases: $500 (for two)
- Removable table: $200
- Bench with storage: $300
- Lighting and decor: $100 **Total**: ~$1,100

Their setup provides a flexible, comfortable space for relaxing, working, and entertaining, both inside and outside the van.

Tips for Designing Your Seating and Living Areas
   Test Layouts: Use temporary furniture or cardboard mock-ups to ensure your design
   feels functional before building permanent structures.
   Think Dual-Purpose: Choose furniture and fixtures that serve multiple roles, like
   seating with storage or tables that convert into beds.
   Prioritize Comfort: Don't underestimate the importance of cushioned seating and
   ergonomic designs for long-term use.
   Maximize Flexibility: Design your living area to adapt to different needs, from
   working and eating to lounging and sleeping.

A well-thought-out seating and living area turns your van into a true home, offering comfort, functionality, and style. With smart design choices and a focus on versatility, you'll create a space where you can relax, work, and entertain—whether you're parked in a quiet forest or a bustling city.

5. Optimize Lighting for Comfort and Functionality

Lighting plays a pivotal role in transforming your van into a welcoming, functional space. The right lighting setup not only enhances comfort and aesthetics but also improves usability, making tasks like cooking, reading, or relaxing easier. By combining ambient, task, and accent lighting, you can create a versatile and energy-efficient system tailored to your van life needs.

Types of Lighting: Building the Perfect Layered Setup

Ambient Lighting
  Purpose: Creates general, evenly distributed light to brighten your living space.
  Options:
  LED Strip Lights: Flexible and easy to install, they provide soft, diffused light along
    walls or ceilings.
  Ceiling Puck Lights: Compact fixtures embedded in the ceiling for a clean, modern
    look.
  Pro Tips:
  Install dimmable lights to adjust brightness based on the time of day or activity.

COMFORT VS. PRACTICALITY

Use warm white LEDs (2700K–3000K) for a cozy and inviting atmosphere.

Task Lighting

Purpose: Provides focused light for specific activities like cooking, reading, or working.

Options:

Under-Cabinet Lights: Illuminate countertops and prep areas in your kitchen.

Adjustable Spotlights: Ideal for reading or working at a desk.

Clip-On Lamps: Portable and versatile, they can be used anywhere in the van.

Pro Tips:

Use cooler white LEDs (4000K–5000K) for better visibility in task-oriented areas.

Place switches in convenient locations for easy access.

Accent Lighting

Purpose: Adds personality and ambiance, making your van feel like a cozy home.

Options:

String Lights: Solar or battery-powered string lights add a whimsical touch.

Backlighting: Place LED strips behind cabinets, shelves, or along the floor for subtle,
  indirect light.

Color-Changing LEDs: Create a dynamic atmosphere with customizable colors for
  different moods.

Pro Tips:

Use accent lighting sparingly to avoid clutter or over-brightening your space.

Solar-powered options are great for conserving energy.

Energy Efficiency: Lighting for Off-Grid Living

When living off-grid, conserving energy is essential. Efficient lighting systems help
you save power without compromising on brightness or functionality.

LED Bulbs:

Consume significantly less power than incandescent or fluorescent bulbs.

Last up to 25 times longer, reducing replacement costs.

Use LEDs rated for 12V systems to integrate seamlessly with your van's battery setup.

Solar-Powered Lights:

Portable solar lanterns or string lights can recharge during the day and provide light at
night.

Great for outdoor use or as a backup option.

Lighting Controls:

Use dimmers to lower power consumption when full brightness isn't needed.

Install motion sensors in areas like closets or under the bed to automatically turn
lights on and off.

Lighting Placement: Strategic and Functional Design

Good lighting placement ensures every corner of your van is usable and visually
appealing.

Ceiling Lights:

COMFORT VS. PRACTICALITY

Place puck lights or LED strips along the ceiling for general illumination.

Use staggered placement to avoid shadows and dark spots.

Under-Cabinet and Shelf Lighting:

Install LED strips under cabinets to brighten work surfaces without needing overhead light.

Use motion-activated lights inside cabinets or drawers for added convenience.

Bedside Lighting:

Add wall-mounted sconces or clip-on reading lamps near your bed for nighttime use.

Install dimmable switches within arm's reach for easy control.

Floor Lighting:

Add LED strips along the floor or steps to improve visibility and safety at night.

Use soft, low-intensity lights to avoid disturbing others if you're sharing the van.

Mood and Seasonal Lighting

Lighting isn't just functional—it can also set the mood and adapt to changing seasons.

Warm Lighting for Winter:

Use warm-toned lights to create a cozy, inviting atmosphere during colder months.

Bright Lighting for Summer:

Use cooler-toned lights to mimic natural daylight and make your space feel fresh.

Holiday and Festive Lighting:

String up small holiday lights or hang decorative lanterns to celebrate special occasions on the road.

DIY Lighting Upgrades

Adding lighting to your van doesn't have to break the bank. With a bit of creativity, you

can enhance your space affordably.

Battery-Powered LED Pucks:

Stick-on lights are easy to install and great for temporary setups or rentals.

PVC or Wooden Light Frames:

Build custom light fixtures using inexpensive materials like PVC pipes or wood.

Smart Lighting Systems:

Use Wi-Fi-enabled lights controlled via smartphone apps for modern convenience.

Real-World Example: A Bright and Functional Lighting Setup

Sophia and Leo, part-time van lifers in their converted Ford Transit, prioritized

lighting for both comfort and efficiency:

- **Ambient Lighting**: Warm LED strip lights run along the ceiling, providing general illumination with a dimmer for adjustable brightness.
- **Task Lighting**: Adjustable spotlights over their kitchen counter and a clip-on reading lamp by the bed.
- **Accent Lighting**: Solar-powered string lights add charm to their living area and double as outdoor lights for evening picnics.
- **Energy Use**: Their 12V LED system draws minimal power, allowing them to stay off-grid for weeks without draining their battery.

Cost Breakdown:

- LED strips and puck lights: $120
- Dimmer switches: $40
- Solar string lights: $25
- Adjustable spotlights: $50 **Total**: ~$235

Tips for Optimizing Lighting in Your Van

Layer Your Lighting: Combine ambient, task, and accent lighting for maximum

versatility.

Prioritize Energy Efficiency: Use LED lights and dimmers to save power for other

essentials.

Test Placement: Temporarily mount lights to find the most effective locations before

committing to permanent installations.

Customize for Your Needs: Focus brighter lights in task areas and softer lighting in

relaxing spaces.

Lighting is more than just a practical necessity—it shapes the way your van feels and functions. With a thoughtful mix of lighting types, strategic placement, and energy-efficient solutions, you can create a space that's both cozy and practical, ready to adapt to any adventure or mood.

6. Control Temperature for Year-Round Comfort

Van life takes you through diverse climates, from chilly mountain mornings to sweltering desert afternoons. Maintaining a comfortable temperature in your van ensures a better experience no matter where you travel. Achieving year-round comfort requires a combination of insulation, ventilation, heating, cooling, and smart temperature control strategies. Here's how to design a system that keeps your van cozy in winter and cool in summer, without overloading your power or budget.

1. Insulation: The Foundation of Temperature Control

Insulation is your first line of defense against extreme temperatures, keeping heat in
during the winter and out during the summer.
Materials for Insulation:
Thinsulate: Lightweight, mold-resistant, and easy to install, making it a favorite
among van lifers.
Foam Board: Rigid foam panels are cost-effective and provide excellent thermal
resistance, ideal for floors and walls.
Reflectix: Works well in small spaces like windows and doors to reflect heat or cold.
Sheep's Wool: A natural, sustainable option that regulates humidity and insulates
effectively.
Areas to Insulate:
Walls and Ceiling: These are the largest surfaces and lose the most heat.
Floor: Adding foam board or underlayment beneath your flooring

reduces cold air
from below.

Windows: Use Reflectix or insulated curtains to block drafts and sunlight.

Tips for Installation:
Seal gaps with expanding foam or caulk to prevent drafts.

Add a vapor barrier in humid climates to protect against moisture buildup.

2. Ventilation: Keeping Air Flowing

Proper ventilation helps maintain fresh air and regulate temperature inside your van.

Roof Vent Fans:
Install a vent fan like the MaxxAir Fan or Fantastic Fan to circulate air and reduce
humidity.

Choose a reversible fan for both intake and exhaust capabilities, allowing you to draw
in cool air or push out hot air.

Cross-Ventilation:
Combine a roof vent with open side windows or vents to create a natural airflow.

Install screened windows to keep bugs out while letting fresh air in.

Floor Vents:
Add floor vents to improve airflow, especially useful in warmer climates where hot air
rises.

Portable Fans:
Use rechargeable or 12V fans to supplement ventilation, especially when parked in
areas without a breeze.

3. Heating: Staying Warm in Winter

Cold weather travel requires an efficient heating system to keep your van warm and comfortable.

Diesel Heaters:

Run off your van's fuel tank or a separate diesel supply.

Pros: Fuel-efficient, heats quickly, and can run for hours on minimal fuel.

Popular Models: Webasto Air Top 2000 or Eberspacher D2.

Propane Heaters:

Use portable models like the Mr. Heater Buddy or fixed units like the Propex HS2000.

Pros: Affordable and widely available fuel.

Cons: Requires ventilation to prevent oxygen depletion and condensation.

Electric Heaters:

Great for those with robust solar and battery systems or access to shore power.

Compact ceramic or infrared heaters are effective for small spaces.

Other Heating Tips:

Use heated blankets or pads for targeted warmth with minimal energy use.

Insulate your sleeping area with heavy-duty sleeping bags or extra blankets.

4. Cooling: Beating the Heat in Summer

Hot weather can make van life uncomfortable, but a few cooling solutions can make all the difference.

Portable Air Conditioners:

Units like the Zero Breeze Mark 2 or EcoFlow Wave provide true cooling but require

    significant power.

Use sparingly in off-grid setups unless you have a large battery bank or access to shore

    power.

Roof Vent Fans:

An absolute must-have for reducing heat buildup, especially when parked in the sun.

Pair with Reflectix window covers to keep sunlight out and temperatures down.

Passive Cooling Strategies:

Park in shaded areas whenever possible.

Use reflective tarps or awnings to create shade around your van.

Leave windows slightly open (with rain guards) to allow heat to escape.

Portable Fans:

Compact, battery-powered fans are perfect for personal cooling and require minimal

    power.

5. Smart Temperature Control Strategies

Beyond heating and cooling devices, there are practical steps you can take to regulate

    your van's temperature year-round.

Block Direct Sunlight:

Install window shades or blackout curtains to reduce heat during the day.

Use Reflectix or thermal shades to insulate windows in extreme temperatures.

Vent Heat at Night:

Open roof vents or windows to release accumulated heat before

sleeping.
Use a small fan to create airflow across your sleeping area.
Layer Clothing:
In cold climates, wear thermal layers and wool socks to stay warm without relying
heavily on heating systems.
Control Humidity:
Use a dehumidifier in cold or humid environments to prevent condensation and
improve overall comfort.
Compact units like Eva-Dry or moisture absorbers like DampRid are effective in small
spaces.

Real-World Example: A Year-Round Temperature-Control Setup
Jenna and Ben, full-time van lifers in their Sprinter van, designed their temperature
control system for comfort in all seasons:

- **Insulation**: Thinsulate in the walls, foam board under the floor, and Reflectix on the windows.
- **Heating**: A Webasto diesel heater keeps the van cozy even during mountain winters.
- **Cooling**: A MaxxAir Fan paired with Reflectix window covers reduces summer heat.
- **Ventilation**: Screened side windows and a floor vent allow for cross-ventilation, even on hot nights.
- **Humidity Control**: An Eva-Dry dehumidifier prevents condensation and keeps their bedding dry.

Cost Breakdown:

- Insulation materials: $700
- Diesel heater: $1,200
- MaxxAir Fan: $300
- Window covers: $150
- Dehumidifier: $70 **Total**: ~$2,420

Their setup enables them to explore snowy peaks and sunny coastlines while staying comfortable year-round.

Tips for Temperature Control Success

Start with Insulation: Proper insulation makes your heating and cooling systems more

effective and energy-efficient.

Invest in Ventilation: A good vent fan is essential for regulating temperature and

humidity.

Plan for Your Climate: Tailor your system to the conditions you'll encounter most

often, such as extreme cold or hot weather.

Test and Adjust: Spend a few nights in your van in different conditions to identify and

address weak points in your temperature control system.

By combining smart design, reliable equipment, and practical strategies, you can create a van that stays comfortable in any season. Whether you're chasing the summer sun or embracing winter adventures, temperature control ensures your van life experience is enjoyable and hassle-free year-round.

7. Add Personal Touches Without Adding Clutter

Your van is your home on wheels, and adding personal touches makes it feel warm, inviting, and uniquely yours. However, in a small space, it's important to balance decoration with practicality. By focusing on functional decor, space-saving design, and lightweight materials, you can infuse your van with personality without creating clutter.

1. Choose Functional Decor

Decor doesn't have to be purely aesthetic—look for items that add beauty *and* utility to
your van.

Throw Blankets and Pillows:
Use soft, colorful throws and cushions to add texture and personality to your living
area.
Opt for lightweight, compact options that double as extra warmth or padding for
seating.

Multi-Use Items:
Example: A decorative basket can store books, electronics, or toiletries while adding
charm.
Wall-mounted hooks can hold jackets, bags, or string lights, keeping them accessible
and off the floor.

Magnetic Accessories:
Magnetic strips for knives, spice jars, or small tools keep these items visible and easy
to reach, while also adding an industrial-chic look.

2. Use Lightweight and Compact Decor

Heavier items increase fuel consumption and make your van harder to handle. Stick to
lightweight materials whenever possible.

Wall Art:
Hang lightweight prints, photos, or fabric wall hangings with removable adhesive
strips or hooks to avoid damaging your walls.

Use corkboards or clipboards for a dynamic display of postcards, notes, or photos that
you can easily change.

Rugs and Mats:
Add a small, washable area rug or floor mat to define your living space and add
warmth underfoot.

Choose low-pile or outdoor-style rugs that are easy to clean and don't trap dirt.

Decorative Lighting:
String lights or battery-powered fairy lights are lightweight, flexible, and create a cozy
atmosphere.

Solar-powered lanterns or LED candles can provide ambiance without adding weight
or requiring wiring.

3. Maximize Vertical Space

In a van, your walls and ceilings are valuable real estate for adding personality and
function.

Hanging Plants:
Use faux plants for zero maintenance or small real plants in macrame

hangers to bring
life to your space.

Secure planters with adhesive or magnetic mounts to prevent movement during travel.

Shelving and Racks:

Install slim, open shelves with a lip to display small decorative items like books,
framed photos, or keepsakes.

Add a wire grid panel for hanging baskets, notes, or lightweight decor.

Ceiling Decor:

Use peel-and-stick ceiling tiles or a fabric canopy for a unique, personalized look.

Install a lightweight overhead shelf near the cab for additional storage that doesn't
feel cluttered.

4. Add Pops of Color and Texture

Incorporating color and texture creates a dynamic, personalized space without
requiring bulky items.

Removable Wallpaper or Decals:

Apply peel-and-stick wallpaper or decals to accent walls or cabinets for an instant
style boost.

Use bold patterns or muted tones to suit your aesthetic.

Curtains and Fabrics:

Hang curtains in fun patterns or colors to add privacy and personality.

Use sheer fabrics for a light, airy feel or blackout curtains for better insulation and
sleep quality.

Bedding and Upholstery:

Choose bedding with vibrant patterns or subtle, calming hues to reflect your style.

Reupholster bench cushions or seats with textured fabrics for a custom touch.

5. Keep It Organized and Clutter-Free

Personal touches should enhance your space, not overwhelm it. Stay organized to

maintain a clean, uncluttered look.

Storage with Style:

Use decorative storage bins or baskets to keep loose items tidy. Look for woven, fabric,

or wooden designs that match your theme.

Opt for stackable or collapsible storage solutions to save space when not in use.

Minimize Collectibles:

Avoid accumulating too many decorative trinkets that can create clutter. Focus on a

few meaningful pieces that spark joy.

Rotating Decor:

Swap out decor seasonally or as your travels inspire new styles. Keeping a minimalist

rotation ensures your van stays fresh without becoming overcrowded.

6. Reflect Your Travels

Use your van as a canvas to showcase your adventures and personal story.

Travel Mementos:

Display souvenirs like postcards, stickers, or small tokens from your destinations.

Create a travel wall or scrapbook to document your journey without cluttering the van.

Maps and Globes:
Add a small map of your route with push pins or markers to track your travels.

Use a compact globe or decorative compass as a stylish nod to your nomadic lifestyle.

Real-World Example: Personalized Yet Practical Decor
Chloe and Max, full-time van lifers in their self-converted Ford Transit, struck the
perfect balance between personality and practicality:

- **Functional Decor**: A woven basket holds their charging cables and books while doubling as a stylish accent piece.
- **Lightweight Art**: They hung framed photos of their favorite travel moments using removable adhesive hooks.
- **Accent Colors**: A mustard yellow throw blanket and teal cushions add pops of color to their gray interior.
- **Travel Wall**: They installed a corkboard where they pin postcards, ticket stubs, and stickers from their adventures.
- **Greenery**: Faux hanging plants bring life to their space without the hassle of maintenance.

Cost Breakdown:

- Peel-and-stick wallpaper: $50
- Decorative storage baskets: $30
- Throw blanket and cushions: $40
- Faux plants and macrame hangers: $25
- Corkboard and pins: $15**Total**: ~$160

COMFORT VS. PRACTICALITY

Their setup reflects their personality and adventures while keeping the van neat and functional.

Tips for Adding Personal Touches Without Clutter

Start Small: Begin with a few key items and add more as you live in your van and

discover what works best.

Think Dual-Purpose: Choose decor that adds functionality, like storage baskets or

multi-use textiles.

Secure Everything: Use adhesives, magnets, or straps to keep decor in place during

travel.

Focus on Meaningful Items: Prioritize pieces that bring you joy or remind you of your

journey.

Adding personal touches is what turns a van into a home. With thoughtful choices and a focus on functionality, you can create a space that reflects your style, celebrates your travels, and remains clutter-free. Whether it's a colorful throw, a travel memento, or a pop of greenery, your decor should make you smile every time you step inside.

8. Keep It Tidy: A Clean Van Feels Bigger

In a small space like a van, clutter can quickly make the area feel cramped and chaotic. Keeping your van tidy isn't just about cleanliness—it's about creating a sense of openness and calm that makes the space feel bigger and more enjoyable to live in. With a little organization, routine maintenance, and smart storage solutions, you can maintain a clean, functional space that's always ready for the next adventure.

1. Declutter Regularly

Van life forces you to live with only the essentials, but even in a minimalist setup,

clutter can creep in.

Purge Unnecessary Items:

Regularly assess what you use and get rid of items you don't need.

For every new item you bring in, try to remove an old one to maintain balance.

Seasonal Storage:

Store out-of-season clothing, gear, or decor in vacuum-sealed bags or bins.

Rotate items based on your travel plans and the climate.

Adopt a "One-Minute Rule":

If tidying up a task will take less than a minute (e.g., putting away shoes or folding a

blanket), do it immediately to prevent clutter from piling up.

2. Organize Your Storage

Efficient storage is the key to maintaining a tidy van.

Categorize Items:

Group similar items together—e.g., kitchen utensils in one drawer, tools in another.

Label containers and bins for easy access.

Use Modular Storage Solutions:

Stackable bins or containers maximize vertical space.

Opt for collapsible or foldable storage that can be tucked away when not in use.

Hidden Storage:
Use under-bed compartments, bench seating with storage, or toe-kick drawers to hide
bulky items like shoes, bedding, or outdoor gear.

Quick-Access Storage:
Install hooks, hanging organizers, or magnetic strips for frequently used items like jackets, keys, or cooking utensils.

3. Clean as You Go
Small messes can quickly overwhelm a small space. Making cleanliness part of your
daily routine keeps your van feeling fresh and inviting.

After Meals:
Wash dishes immediately after eating to prevent buildup in the sink or countertop.

Wipe down counters and the stove to avoid grease and crumbs accumulating.

Daily Sweeps:
Spend five minutes each evening tidying up—putting items back in their place,
sweeping the floor, and folding blankets.

Use a small handheld vacuum or dustpan and brush for quick cleanups.

Control Trash:
Empty trash and recycling bins regularly to prevent odors and overflow.

Use small, lidded trash cans or compost bags to contain waste.

4. Manage Dirt and Dust
With the constant in-and-out movement of van life, dirt and dust

are inevitable.

Minimize their impact with these strategies:

Shoes Off Policy:

Designate a spot near the door for shoes, such as a small mat or basket.

Consider using slip-on shoes or sandals for quick exits and entries.

Floor Protection:

Use a washable, durable rug to catch dirt and protect your floors.

Consider a boot tray for muddy or wet shoes.

Dust Prevention:

Use microfiber cloths to dust surfaces regularly.

Close windows and vents during windy or dusty conditions to minimize debris inside.

5. Keep Your Bed Made

In a small space, an unmade bed can make the entire van feel untidy.

Daily Bed-Making Routine:

Make your bed every morning as part of your routine. It instantly makes your space

look cleaner and more organized.

Streamline Bedding:

Use a fitted sheet, a single duvet, and a couple of pillows for easy maintenance.

Choose bedding materials that are easy to clean and don't wrinkle easily.

6. Control Odors

A clean van isn't just about appearance—it's also about keeping it smelling fresh.

Air Circulation:

Use roof vent fans or open windows to keep fresh air circulating.

Add an air purifier or dehumidifier in humid climates to reduce musty smells.

Neutralize Odors:
Place activated charcoal bags or baking soda containers in odor-prone areas like the
kitchen, bathroom, or shoe storage.
Use natural air fresheners like essential oil diffusers or citrus peels.

Clean Surfaces:
Regularly clean areas that trap smells, like trash bins, the fridge, and your sink.

7. Create Systems for Maintenance

Consistency is the key to keeping your van tidy over time.

Weekly Deep Clean:
Dedicate time each week for a more thorough clean, including wiping down surfaces,
reorganizing storage, and vacuuming.

Travel Cleanup Routine:
Before hitting the road, secure loose items, empty trash bins, and make sure
everything is stored properly.
Use bungee cords or Velcro straps to prevent shifting during travel.

Checklist for Campsites:
Before leaving a campsite, do a quick cleanup of your van and surrounding area to
ensure you're leaving no trace and starting your next journey with a clean slate.

Real-World Example: Tidy Van Success

Lucy and Mark, a couple living in their converted Ram ProMaster, keep their van
feeling spacious and clean with these habits:

- **Daily Habits**: Shoes are always removed at the door, and they clean up after every meal.
- **Smart Storage**: A pull-out drawer under their bed holds their shoes and outdoor gear, while labeled bins keep their kitchen organized.
- **Odor Control**: Activated charcoal bags in their trash can and fridge prevent unpleasant smells.
- **Cleaning Tools**: A handheld vacuum and microfiber cloths are always within reach for quick cleanups.

Cost Breakdown:

- Shoe mat: $15
- Handheld vacuum: $40
- Activated charcoal bags: $20
- Storage bins: $30
- Microfiber cloths: $10 **Total**: ~$115

Their small investment in cleaning tools and organization keeps their van tidy and enjoyable, no matter how long they stay on the road.

Tips for Keeping Your Van Tidy

   Make It a Habit: Incorporate tidying into your daily routine so it feels natural and

   effortless.

   Designate a Place for Everything: Assign specific spots for all your belongings to

   prevent clutter from building up.

   Stay Flexible: Be willing to adjust your organization systems as your needs evolve.

   Enjoy the Benefits: A clean, tidy van feels more spacious, reduces stress, and lets you focus on enjoying van life to the fullest.

By keeping your van clean and organized, you create a space that feels bigger, brighter, and more inviting. With consistent habits and a few simple tools, your van can be a sanctuary of order and calm, ready for whatever adventure comes next.

5

Home Comforts

Your van isn't just a vehicle; it's your home. While the allure of van life often lies in adventure and minimalism, creating a space that feels cozy, personal, and functional is key to long-term happiness on the road. From the essentials that make life easier to the small touches that bring joy, this chapter explores how to turn your van into a true sanctuary.

1. Define What "Home" Means to You

Before you start transforming your van into a home, take a moment to reflect on what "home" truly means to you. Everyone's idea of home is deeply personal, shaped by past experiences, favorite spaces, and what makes them feel safe and comfortable. For some, home is a cozy retreat where they can curl up with a book. For others, it's a functional space where they can cook, work, or entertain. Understanding your unique needs and priorities will guide the design and organization of your van, ensuring it reflects your lifestyle and values.

1 What Do You Miss About Traditional Homes?

Think about the spaces you've lived in before. What made them feel like home, and
what do you miss most?

Comfort:
Do you value a cozy bed, a favorite chair, or a spot to relax after a long day?
Consider making your sleeping area a top priority if comfort is your focus.

Functionality:
Do you miss having a well-equipped kitchen or a dedicated workspace?
If so, plan for a functional cooking area or a desk that allows you to stay productive.

Atmosphere:
Is it the warmth of soft lighting, the presence of personal mementos, or the feeling of
privacy that makes a space feel like home?
Prioritize decor, ambiance, and privacy solutions to recreate this atmosphere.

2 What Activities Bring You Joy and Comfort?

Your van should support the activities that make you happy and grounded. Ask
yourself:

What Do You Do to Relax?
If you love reading, make space for books and a cozy reading nook.
If you enjoy watching movies, add a small projector or tablet stand for entertainment.

What Keeps You Active?
If you're into outdoor activities, prioritize storage for your gear, like

bikes, kayaks, or
   hiking equipment.

If yoga or exercise is your thing, create a flexible open space for stretching or
   workouts.

What Makes You Feel Productive?

Include a functional workspace with enough light and storage for your tools, electronics, or creative supplies.

3 How Can Your Van Reflect Your Personality?

Your home is an extension of who you are, and your van should reflect that.

Decorative Touches:

Include colors, patterns, or materials that resonate with you. If you love nature, add
   earthy tones, wood accents, or hanging plants.

Use photos, artwork, or small mementos that remind you of family, friends, or past
   adventures.

Showcase Your Interests:

Are you an artist? Set up a small art station.

A music lover? Find a way to store and display your guitar or favorite records.

Create a Signature Space:

Designate one area of your van that's completely "yours"—a place that feels like your
   personal sanctuary.

4 Plan for Emotional Comfort

Feeling "at home" isn't just about physical items; it's also about emotional well being.

Privacy:
Add blackout curtains or insulated window covers to create a sense of privacy and
security.
Choose campsites or parking spots that make you feel safe and relaxed.

Connection:
If staying connected to loved ones is important, ensure your van has reliable Wi-Fi or
cellular service for video calls or messaging.
Create spaces where you can host or entertain friends if community is a priority.

Routines:
Develop daily rituals like morning coffee at your fold-out table or journaling in your
bed. These habits help you feel grounded no matter where you are.

Real-World Example: Redefining Home on the Road
Emily, a solo traveler, knew that home for her meant comfort, creativity, and
connection. Here's how she translated that into her van setup:

- **Comfort**: She invested in a plush mattress and cozy bedding for her fixed bed, creating a relaxing retreat for reading and journaling.
- **Creativity**: She added a foldable desk near the window for painting and sketching, with storage for her art supplies.
- **Connection**: Emily hung photos of her family on a magnetic board and made space for a small Bluetooth speaker to play her favorite music.

For Emily, home wasn't just a place—it was a feeling, and her van became the perfect expression of it.

Tips for Defining "Home" in Your Van
Start with Essentials: Focus on what you can't live without, like a comfortable bed or a
functional kitchen.
Keep It Flexible: Allow your van to evolve as your needs and lifestyle change.
Make It Personal: Incorporate small details that remind you of what makes you happy
and grounded.
Embrace Minimalism: Avoid overloading your van with unnecessary items; instead,
focus on a few meaningful touches that bring joy.

By taking the time to define what "home" means to you, you can create a van that isn't just a vehicle but a sanctuary. Whether it's comfort, creativity, or connection that matters most, designing with intention ensures your space reflects who you are and supports the lifestyle you love.

2. Create a Cozy Sleeping Space

Your sleeping area is more than just a place to rest—it's a sanctuary where you recharge after long days on the road. A well-designed, cozy sleeping space can make your van feel like home, turning even the smallest space into a haven of comfort and relaxation. Here's how to create a restful and functional sleeping area tailored to your needs.

1 Invest in a Comfortable Bed

Your bed is the centerpiece of your sleeping space, and getting it right is essential.

Mattress Choices:

Memory Foam: Conforms to your body, providing excellent support and pressure

relief. Cut it to fit odd dimensions in your van.

Latex Foam: A natural, breathable option that resists moisture and allergens.

Hybrid Mattresses: Combine foam and springs for additional support in larger vans.

Folding Mattresses: Perfect for convertible setups where the bed doubles as a sofa or

dinette.

Tips for a Better Sleep Setup:

Use a mattress topper for added comfort, especially if you're repurposing an existing

mattress.

Elevate your mattress on slats to allow airflow and prevent moisture buildup.

2 Choose Bedding That Enhances Comfort

The right bedding makes all the difference in creating a cozy environment.

Sheets and Blankets:

Use soft, breathable fabrics like bamboo, cotton, or microfiber.

Layer lightweight sheets with a down or synthetic comforter for year-round

versatility.

Add a weighted blanket for extra comfort during colder months.

Pillows:

Choose supportive, high-quality pillows tailored to your sleeping position.

Consider memory foam or down-alternative options for compact and travel-friendly

designs.

Storage-Friendly Bedding:

Opt for compact, packable options like compressible sleeping bags or vacuum-sealed

duvets.

Use pillowcases with zippers or hidden compartments for extra storage of small items.

3 Optimize the Layout for Comfort and Functionality

Your sleeping area should be designed to maximize comfort while making the most of

your space.

Bed Configurations:

Fixed Bed: A permanent setup that's always ready for sleep. Ideal for larger vans where

storage can be built underneath.

Convertible Bed: Transforms into a sofa, dinette, or workspace during the day. Perfect

for smaller vans.

Murphy Bed: Folds up against the wall to save space while providing a full-sized

sleeping surface.

Maximize Bed Accessibility:

If space allows, align your bed lengthwise with the van to avoid climbing over a

partner.

Use steps or a ladder if your bed is elevated for storage.

Ventilation:
Place your bed near a window or roof vent for fresh air circulation. A small fan can also
improve airflow.

4 Add Ambiance with Lighting

Soft, adjustable lighting transforms your sleeping area into a cozy retreat.

LED Strip Lights:
Install dimmable LED strips along the ceiling or under cabinets for a warm, ambient
glow.

Reading Lights:
Add clip-on or wall-mounted reading lamps with adjustable brightness for late-night
reading.

Accent Lighting:
Use fairy lights, small lanterns, or battery-powered candles to create a relaxing
atmosphere.

5 Enhance Privacy and Noise Control

Privacy and quiet are essential for restful sleep, especially in busy areas or campsites.

Blackout Curtains:
Hang heavy-duty curtains or use insulated window covers to block light and noise.

Soundproofing:
Add foam insulation or sound-deadening mats to walls and doors to reduce outside
noise.

White Noise Machines:
A small white noise device or app can help drown out background sounds.

6 Keep It Clean and Organized

A tidy sleeping area feels more restful and welcoming.

Under-Bed Storage:
Use bins or pull-out drawers to store extra blankets, clothing, or gear.

Overhead Shelving:
Install slim, enclosed shelves for small items like books, electronics, or toiletries.

Nightstand Alternatives:
Use wall-mounted pouches or baskets to keep essentials like your phone, glasses, or
water bottle within reach.

7 Personalize Your Sleeping Space

Make your bed feel like home by adding touches that reflect your personality and style.

Decorative Throw Pillows:
Choose pillows in your favorite colors or patterns to add visual interest.

Photos and Art:
Hang lightweight frames or use magnetic boards to display photos and mementos.

Aromatherapy:
Use essential oils or a portable diffuser to create a calming scent like lavender or
eucalyptus.

Real-World Example: A Cozy Sleeping Setup

Lena and Jake, a couple living in their DIY-built Ford Transit, created a comfortable
and stylish sleeping area:

- **Bed**: A fixed queen-size platform bed with a memory foam mattress and slatted base for ventilation.
- **Bedding**: Soft bamboo sheets, a weighted blanket, and compressible pillows for easy storage.
- **Ambiance**: Warm LED strip lights run along the headboard, and blackout curtains provide privacy and insulation.
- **Storage**: Under-bed drawers hold their off-season clothing and extra blankets, while wall-mounted baskets keep their phones and books accessible.

Cost Breakdown:

- Memory foam mattress: $400
- Bedding and pillows: $150
- Blackout curtains: $50
- LED lighting: $40**Total**: ~$640

Their setup provides a cozy retreat for restful nights, with enough storage to keep the space clean and uncluttered.

Tips for Creating a Cozy Sleeping Space
Prioritize Comfort: Invest in a high-quality mattress and bedding—it's worth it for
better sleep.
Keep It Tidy: Regularly make your bed and store extra items to maintain a clean,
inviting space.

Adapt to the Seasons: Use layers for year-round comfort, swapping lightweight

fabrics in summer for heavier blankets in winter.

Add Your Style: Personalize your sleeping area with decor and colors that make you

feel at home.

With thoughtful design and a focus on comfort, your sleeping space can become the heart of your van—a peaceful, personal retreat that feels like home no matter where you park.

3. Design a Functional Kitchen

A well-designed kitchen can elevate your van life experience, making it easy to prepare meals, store food, and clean up efficiently. No matter the size of your space, thoughtful planning and smart choices can transform your van kitchen into a practical and enjoyable workspace. Here's how to create a functional kitchen tailored to your cooking style and storage needs.

1 Choose the Right Cooking Appliances

Your choice of cooking appliances will depend on your energy setup, space availability,

and the type of meals you enjoy preparing.

- **Stoves**:
- **Propane Stoves**: Portable or built-in dual-burner stoves are versatile and easy to use.
- Example: Coleman Triton or Camp Chef Everest for reliable performance.

- **Butane Stoves**: Lightweight and compact, great for occasional cooking.
- **Induction Cooktops**: Perfect for vans with robust solar and battery systems, offering clean, flameless cooking.
- **Ovens**:
- Consider a small propane oven if you love baking or roasting. Options like the Camp Chef Outdoor Oven are popular among van lifers.
- Alternatively, use a stovetop Dutch oven for baking bread or casseroles.
- **Microwaves**:
- Compact models are ideal for quick reheating if you frequently stay at campsites with shore power or have a high-capacity battery setup.

2 Maximize Storage for Food and Cooking Essentials

Efficient storage keeps your kitchen organized and functional.

Dry Goods and Pantry:

Install pull-out pantry shelves or stackable bins for easy access to staples like rice,

pasta, and canned goods.

Use airtight containers to keep food fresh and pest-free.

Refrigeration:

12V Compressor Fridges: Energy-efficient and ideal for off-grid living. Popular

models include the Dometic CFX series and ARB Elements.

Coolers: A budget-friendly alternative for short trips, though they require regular ice

replenishment.

Utensils and Cookware:

Use drawer organizers to neatly store utensils.

Opt for nesting or collapsible pots, pans, and bowls to save space.

Install magnetic strips for knives or hang hooks for spatulas and ladles.

Cleaning Supplies:

Designate a small bin or drawer for dish soap, sponges, and microfiber cloths.

Use collapsible drying racks or mats to save counter space.

3 Optimize Counter Space for Meal Prep

Counter space is at a premium in van kitchens, so smart design is essential.

Foldable Extensions:

Add a flip-up countertop that extends your workspace when needed and folds away

when not in use.

Example: Install one near the sink for prepping vegetables or drying dishes.

Stowable Cutting Boards:

Use a cutting board that fits over your sink or stove to create additional prep space.

Multi-Purpose Surfaces:

Choose a sink with a cover that doubles as a flat prep area when not in use.

4 Include a Functional Sink and Water System

A reliable sink setup makes cooking and cleaning more efficient.

Sink Options:

Single-Basin Stainless Steel Sink: Durable, easy to clean, and compact.

Collapsible or Portable Sink: Great for ultra-minimalist setups.

Water Systems:

Foot Pump: Simple, energy-free, and ideal for conserving water.

12V Electric Pump: Provides running water with minimal effort, perfect for more

advanced setups.

Grey water Management:

Install a greywater tank under the sink to collect wastewater for responsible disposal.

Use biodegradable soap to minimize environmental impact.

5 Plan for Energy Efficiency

Running a kitchen off-grid requires careful attention to energy use.

Appliance Choices:

Use 12V appliances designed for off-grid living to minimize power consumption.

Look for energy-efficient models of fridges, stoves, and fans.

Conserve Energy While Cooking:

Use lids on pots and pans to speed up cooking times.

Batch-cook meals and store leftovers for quick reheating later.

Lighting:

Install task lighting under cabinets or along the ceiling to illuminate prep areas

without wasting energy.

6 Add Personal Touches to Make it Yours

Your kitchen should be as much about personality as practicality.

Decorative Storage:

Use glass jars or metal tins for storing spices and dry goods to add a rustic or modern

touch.

Hang a colorful fruit hammock to brighten the space while keeping produce fresh.

Travel-Inspired Decor:
Display magnets, stickers, or small souvenirs from your adventures on your fridge or
backsplash.
Use patterned tiles or peel-and-stick backsplashes to reflect your style.

Real-World Example: A Functional Van Kitchen

Alyssa and John, full-time van lifers in a converted Mercedes Sprinter, created a
highly functional kitchen setup that meets all their cooking and storage needs:

- **Cooking Appliances**: A built-in propane stove with two burners and a small convection oven for baking.
- **Refrigeration**: A Dometic CFX3 45L fridge, which runs off their 200Ah lithium battery system.
- **Storage**: Pull-out pantry shelves for dry goods, a magnetic strip for knives, and hanging baskets for produce.
- **Water System**: A stainless steel sink with a 12V electric pump and a 7-gallon greywater tank.
- **Personal Touches**: A backsplash made of travel-inspired peel-and-stick tiles and a spice rack featuring jars labeled with handwritten tags.

Cost Breakdown:

- Stove and oven: $400
- Fridge: $900
- Sink and plumbing: $250
- Storage upgrades: $150

- Decor: $50**Total**: ~$1,750

Their kitchen allows them to prepare everything from quick breakfasts to gourmet dinners, all while staying organized and energy-efficient.

Tips for Designing a Functional Kitchen

Plan for Your Cooking Style: Tailor your kitchen to the meals you'll actually make

minimalists may not need a full stove, while foodies might prioritize an oven.

Maximize Vertical Space: Install shelves, hooks, and racks to make the most of every

inch.

Stay Flexible: Choose portable or collapsible items that adapt to different needs and

save space.

Keep It Tidy: Clean as you go to avoid clutter and make cooking a pleasant experience.

A functional kitchen is at the heart of van life, making it easy to enjoy fresh meals and stay self-sufficient on the road. With thoughtful design and creative storage solutions, your van kitchen can be practical, efficient, and full of personality.

4. Stay Comfortable in Any Climate

Van life means embracing diverse environments, from snowy mountaintops to sunny deserts. Staying comfortable year-round requires thoughtful planning for heating, cooling, ventilation, and insulation. With the right tools and strategies, you can transform your van into a climate-controlled oasis, no matter where your travels take you.

1 Insulate Your Van for Temperature Regulation

Proper insulation is the foundation of climate comfort, helping to maintain a stable

interior temperature while reducing energy needs.

Best Insulation Materials:

Thinsulate: Lightweight, moisture-resistant, and easy to install. Excellent for walls,

ceilings, and floors.

Foam Board: Ideal for floors and walls, offering high thermal resistance and

durability.

Reflectix: Great for window coverings to reflect heat in summer and retain warmth in

winter.

Sheep's Wool: Natural, breathable, and sustainable, with excellent moisture

regulation.

Key Areas to Insulate:

Walls and Ceilings: Insulate large surfaces to reduce heat loss or gain.

Floors: Add foam board under the flooring to prevent cold from seeping in.

Windows: Use custom-fit Reflectix or insulated curtains for additional thermal

protection.

Tips for Installation:

Seal gaps and cracks with expanding foam or caulk to prevent drafts.

Add a vapor barrier in humid climates to protect against condensation.

2 Heating Solutions for Cold Weather

Keeping your van warm during winter adventures is essential for comfort and safety.

Diesel Heaters:

Run on your van's fuel supply or a separate diesel tank. Efficient and reliable for

consistent heat.

Popular Models: Webasto Air Top 2000 and Eberspacher D2.

Pros: Minimal fuel consumption and effective for all-night heating.

Cons: Higher upfront cost and professional installation recommended.

Propane Heaters:

Compact and portable, propane heaters like the Mr. Heater Buddy are affordable and

effective.

Safety Tips: Ensure proper ventilation to avoid oxygen depletion and condensation.

Electric Heaters:

Best for those with shore power access or robust battery systems. Compact ceramic or

infrared heaters provide safe, flameless warmth.

Low-Tech Solutions:

Use heated blankets or sleeping bags rated for cold temperatures.

Insulate your bed area with extra blankets or thermal curtains.

3 Cooling Strategies for Hot Weather

Managing heat in your van is critical for summer travel, especially in sunny or humid climates.

Ventilation Fans:
Roof-mounted fans like the MaxxAir Fan or Fantastic Fan provide excellent airflow
and reduce interior temperatures.
Use reversible fans to pull in cool air or push out hot air depending on the time of day.

Portable Air Conditioners:
Options like the Zero Breeze Mark 2 or EcoFlow Wave offer effective cooling but
require significant power.
Best suited for vans with large battery banks or access to shore power.

Passive Cooling Techniques:
Park in shaded areas and use Reflectix window covers to block direct sunlight.
Open windows and vents to create cross-breezes, especially at night.
Hang a light-colored tarp or awning to reduce heat buildup inside your van.

Portable Fans:
Battery-operated or USB-powered fans provide localized cooling with minimal energy
consumption.

4 Manage Humidity and Condensation

Controlling humidity is essential for maintaining a comfortable and mold-free living
space.

Dehumidifiers:
Compact units like the Eva-Dry or electric models help reduce moisture in humid
climates.

Moisture Absorbers:
Affordable solutions like DampRid or silica gel packs work well in small spaces.

Ventilation:
Proper airflow through roof fans and windows minimizes condensation.

Insulation:
Prevents interior surfaces from reaching temperatures where moisture condenses.

5 Maintain a Comfortable Bed Temperature

Your bed's comfort level directly affects how well you sleep in extreme temperatures.

For Winter:
Add a heated mattress pad or an insulated sleeping bag for cozy nights.
Use flannel sheets and thick blankets to trap heat.

For Summer:
Use cooling gel toppers and breathable cotton or bamboo sheets to wick moisture and
regulate temperature.
Position a small fan near your bed to improve airflow while sleeping.

Real-World Example: Climate Control Success

Emily and Sean, full-time van lifers in a converted Sprinter van, travel year-round
through diverse climates. Here's how they stay comfortable:

- **Insulation**: Thinsulate throughout the walls and ceiling, foam board under the floor, and Reflectix on all windows.
- **Heating**: A Webasto diesel heater keeps them warm during ski

season with minimal fuel consumption.
- **Cooling**: A MaxxAir Fan paired with Reflectix covers and an awning creates a cool, shaded space in summer.
- **Humidity Control**: An Eva-Dry dehumidifier and cross-ventilation prevent condensation in humid areas.
- **Bedding**: Flannel sheets and a heated blanket for winter, paired with bamboo sheets and a cooling topper for summer.

Cost Breakdown:

- Insulation: $800
- Diesel heater: $1,200
- MaxxAir Fan: $300
- Dehumidifier: $70
- Bedding upgrades: $150 **Total**: ~$2,520

Their setup allows them to explore snowy mountains and sunny beaches with equal comfort, proving that a well-designed van can handle any climate.

Tips for Staying Comfortable in Any Climate

Invest in Insulation First: Good insulation reduces reliance on heating and cooling
   devices.

Prioritize Ventilation: A quality roof fan is essential for year-round comfort and air
   circulation.

Adapt to Conditions: Carry gear and clothing suited to your expected climates, from
   thermal layers to sun hats.

Test Your Setup: Spend a few nights in varied weather to identify and

fix any weak
  points in your climate control system.

By planning for insulation, heating, cooling, and humidity control, you can create a van that's ready for all seasons. Whether you're escaping the summer heat or chasing snow-covered peaks, your van will be a comfortable and welcoming retreat.

5. Add Personal Touches

Turning your van into a home isn't just about functionality—it's about making it feel like yours. Adding personal touches can transform even the simplest van into a warm, inviting space that reflects your personality, style, and journey. By combining thoughtful decor, meaningful mementos, and a bit of creativity, you can make your van a true home on wheels without adding clutter.

1 Showcase Your Style with Decor
  Decorative elements can set the tone for your van, creating a space that feels
    comfortable and uniquely yours.
  Colors and Patterns:
    Choose a color palette that feels soothing or energizing, depending on your style.
    Neutral tones with pops of color, earthy shades, or bold patterns can all create a sense
      of harmony.
    Use textiles like throw pillows, blankets, or curtains to incorporate color and texture.
  Wall Art:

Hang lightweight art prints, framed photos, or tapestries using removable adhesive
hooks.

Create a rotating gallery of postcards or travel photos on a magnetic board or
corkboard.

Rugs and Mats:

Add a small area rug or runner to define your living space and make it feel cozier.

Choose materials that are easy to clean, like flat-woven or outdoor rugs.

2 Decorate with Meaningful Items

Surrounding yourself with meaningful items can bring comfort and joy to your space.

Travel Mementos:

Display souvenirs, like small figurines, shells, or local crafts, from places you've
visited.

Create a scrapbook or map wall to document your journey and track your travels.

Family and Friends:

Hang photos of loved ones or pets to feel connected, no matter where you are.

Use digital photo frames to rotate through a collection of pictures without taking up
space.

Inspirational Touches:

Include a vision board, quotes, or affirmations on your walls or desk to keep you
motivated and focused.

3 Add Greenery and Natural Elements

Plants and natural materials can make your van feel more alive and grounded.

Real Plants:

Choose low-maintenance plants like succulents, pothos, or snake plants.

Use small pots with secure bases or macramé hangers to prevent spills.

Faux Plants:

If you don't want the hassle of maintenance, faux greenery can provide the same

aesthetic with zero upkeep.

Natural Materials:

Incorporate wood accents, woven baskets, or stone coasters for a touch of nature in

your design.

4 Create a Cozy Ambiance with Lighting

Lighting is one of the easiest ways to personalize your van and create a cozy

atmosphere.

String Lights:

Use solar-powered or USB string lights to add a soft glow to your living area or bed.

Accent Lighting:

Install LED strip lights under shelves, around windows, or along the ceiling for warm,

indirect light.

Portable Lamps:

Use rechargeable lanterns or battery-powered candles for flexible, cozy lighting options.

5 Incorporate Your Hobbies and Passions

Your van should reflect the activities and interests that bring you joy.

Music:

Store your guitar, ukulele, or other instruments in a secure, easily accessible spot.

Use Bluetooth speakers or headphones to enjoy your favorite playlists.

Art and Crafts:

Keep art supplies, sketchbooks, or knitting tools in a dedicated storage area.

Include a small fold-out table or desk to create a functional workspace.

Books and Games:

Install a small bookshelf or use fabric pockets to hold your favorite reads.

Keep a deck of cards or compact board games for entertainment on rainy days.

5.6 Personalize Functional Areas

Even practical parts of your van, like the kitchen or bathroom, can reflect your style.

Kitchen:

Use decorative jars or tins for storing spices and dry goods.

Add a patterned backsplash or colorful dish towels to brighten up the space.

Bathroom:

Choose soft, colorful hand towels and hang a small piece of art or a mirror for a more
   polished feel.

Real-World Example: Personalizing a Van
Clara, a solo traveler in her self-built Ford Transit, created a van that feels uniquely hers:

- **Decor**: A neutral base of white walls and wood accents with pops of turquoise and yellow in her pillows, rug, and curtains.
- **Mementos**: A corkboard displaying postcards from her travels and a shelf of small souvenirs.
- **Greenery**: A hanging pothos plant in the kitchen and a faux succulent on her desk.
- **Lighting**: Solar-powered string lights around her bed and warm LED strip lights along the ceiling.
- **Hobbies**: A small guitar stored on a wall-mounted hanger and a foldable easel for painting outdoors.

Cost Breakdown:

- Decorative textiles: $80
- Corkboard and pins: $20
- Faux and real plants: $30
- String lights and LED strips: $40
- Guitar hanger and art supplies: $50**Total**: ~$220

Her thoughtful touches turned her van into a space that feels personal, creative, and full of life.

Tips for Adding Personal Touches Without Adding Clutter
  Choose Multi-Functional Decor: Opt for items that serve both

aesthetic and practical

purposes, like storage baskets or decorative jars.

Secure Everything: Use adhesives, straps, or hooks to keep items in place during

travel.

Rotate Items: Swap out decor or mementos seasonally to keep your space fresh

without overcrowding.

Focus on Quality Over Quantity: Select a few meaningful pieces instead of

overwhelming the space with too many items.

By adding personal touches to your van, you can create a space that feels not only functional but also warm, welcoming, and reflective of your unique journey. From greenery and lighting to mementos and hobbies, these small details make your van a true home on wheels.

6. Prioritize Comfort in Daily Living

Comfort is essential to making your van feel like home. While van life may come with compromises, designing your space to support daily routines and relaxation ensures your time on the road remains enjoyable. By incorporating thoughtful seating, entertainment, and practical solutions for daily activities, you can create a van that caters to your needs without sacrificing comfort.

1 Design a Comfortable Seating Area

A versatile and comfortable seating area can serve as a lounge, dining space, and work

zone.

Cushioned Seating:
Use high-density foam cushions with durable, washable covers for long-lasting
comfort.
Add throw pillows for back support and a touch of style.
Swivel Seats:
Install swivel bases on your van's front seats to incorporate them into your living area.
Use seat covers with extra padding for added comfort.
Bench Seating with Storage:
Build a bench with a hinged lid or drawers underneath to double as a storage space for
blankets, shoes, or gear.
Portable Seating:
Keep lightweight folding chairs or stools on hand for both indoor and outdoor use.

2 Create a Space for Relaxation

Van life isn't all about movement—having a space to unwind is crucial.

Lounging Area:
Designate a cozy nook with a small rug, cushions, or a beanbag for relaxing, reading,
or meditating.
Install a hammock or sling seat for a unique, space-saving lounge option.
Lighting:
Use dimmable LED lights or warm string lights to create a calming ambiance in the
evenings.
Entertainment Zone:

Mount a tablet or small TV for movie nights, or invest in a compact projector for a
cinematic experience on the go.
Add a Bluetooth speaker for music, podcasts, or audiobooks.

3 Ensure a Functional Dining Setup

Mealtime should be comfortable and enjoyable, whether you're parked at a scenic spot
or hunkered down during bad weather.

Foldable Tables:
Use a wall-mounted or removable pedestal table for indoor dining.
Choose a design that can double as a desk or prep area.

Outdoor Dining Options:
Keep a portable camping table and chairs stored in your van for alfresco meals.
Add an awning or tarp for shade and weather protection.

Tableware:
Opt for durable, lightweight dishes and utensils, such as melamine or stainless steel.
Store essentials like plates, cups, and cutlery in easy-to-access drawers or bins.

4 Plan for Cleanliness and Hygiene

Staying clean and organized contributes significantly to daily comfort.

Bathroom Setup:
Include a portable toilet, composting toilet, or bucket system for convenience and
hygiene.
Use a privacy curtain or pop-up tent for added discretion if needed.

Showers:

Consider a solar shower bag or portable shower system for quick outdoor rinses.
Install a retractable curtain near the rear doors for a makeshift outdoor shower area.

Hygiene Accessories:
Store toiletries in a hanging organizer or small tote to keep them contained.
Use quick-dry towels and keep a small mirror mounted or stored for grooming.

5 Create Efficient Work and Hobbies Spaces

If you work remotely or enjoy hobbies, dedicate a functional area for these activities.

Workspace Setup:
Use a fold-out desk, a pull-out drawer, or a small table as a workspace.
Install an ergonomic chair or use cushions for proper seating support during work sessions.

Hobby Storage:
Dedicate space for hobby supplies like art materials, cameras, or sports gear.
Keep items organized in bins, shelves, or hanging storage to avoid clutter.

Power Access:
Position your workspace near USB outlets or a power strip for easy charging of devices.

6 Manage Temperature for Daily Comfort

Daily living becomes much easier when your van is comfortable in all weather conditions.

Heating:
Use a diesel heater, propane heater, or portable electric heater for cold mornings or
  evenings.
Keep a cozy blanket or heated throw nearby for added warmth.
Cooling:
Use a roof vent fan, portable fan, or evaporative cooler to stay comfortable in hot
  climates.
Park in shaded areas and use reflective window covers to minimize heat buildup.
Ventilation:
Open windows and doors to create airflow while parked, and use bug screens to keep
  insects out.

7 Add Personal Touches to Daily Routines

Infuse your daily activities with small comforts that make van life feel special.

Morning Rituals:
Set up a coffee or tea station with your favorite mug, a French press, or a compact
  kettle.
Create a relaxing morning routine with yoga or meditation in a designated space.

Evening Wind-Down:
Use soft lighting and soothing music to create a relaxing atmosphere before bed.
Keep a favorite book, journal, or deck of cards within reach for quiet evenings.

Real-World Example: Comfortable Daily Living
Nina and Alex, part-time van lifers in their converted Ram ProMaster, designed their
van for maximum daily comfort:

- **Seating**: Swivel front seats paired with a cushioned bench create a comfortable lounge area.
- **Dining**: A removable pedestal table serves as both a dining and workspace.
- **Relaxation**: LED string lights and a Bluetooth speaker set the mood for cozy evenings.
- **Hygiene**: A portable toilet stored under their bench and a solar shower bag attached to the rear doors ensure cleanliness on the road.
- **Work Zone**: A fold-out desk and ergonomic chair make remote work seamless.

Cost Breakdown:

- Swivel seat bases: $500 (for two)
- Portable toilet: $100
- Solar shower bag: $30
- Table and workspace setup: $200
- Lighting and decor: $80**Total**: ~$910

Their setup allows them to cook, work, relax, and stay clean without feeling cramped or uncomfortable.

Tips for Prioritizing Comfort in Daily Living
Invest in Versatile Furniture: Swivel seats, foldable tables, and multi-functional

benches maximize comfort without taking up space.

Make Cleanliness Easy: Keep hygiene supplies organized and accessible to maintain a
fresh living environment.

Adapt to Your Needs: Tailor your van to your daily habits, from workspaces to
lounging areas.

Create Comfort Zones: Dedicate specific areas for relaxation, dining, and work to keep
your van functional and enjoyable.

By prioritizing comfort in daily living, you'll create a van that feels as inviting and practical as any home. Thoughtful seating, efficient spaces, and small touches of luxury ensure that every day on the road is as comfortable as it is adventurous.

7. Build Community on the Road

While van life is often associated with freedom and solitude, building connections with others can make the experience even more enriching. Whether you're seeking fellow van lifers, local communities, or shared interests, forming relationships on the road can provide support, inspiration, and a sense of belonging. Here's how to foster community while still enjoying the independence of van life.

1 Connect with Fellow Van Lifers

The van life community is a welcoming network of like-minded travelers who share
tips, stories, and camaraderie.

Attend Van Life Gatherings:

Events like Vanlife Diaries meetups, Descend on Bend, or smaller regional gatherings
are great opportunities to meet others and exchange ideas.
Many of these events include workshops, group activities, and opportunities to share
skills.

Join Online Communities:
Facebook groups, forums, and subreddits like r/VanLife are excellent resources for
connecting with fellow travelers.
Apps like **iOverlander**, **Campendium**, or **Vanlife App** not only help find campsites but
also highlight places where other van lifers are parked.

Use Social Media:
Follow hashtags like #VanLife or #HomeOnWheels to discover and connect with
others.
Share your own journey and engage with others by commenting on posts or direct
messaging.

2 Participate in Local Communities

Building relationships with locals adds depth to your travel experience and helps you
feel connected to the places you visit.

Volunteer:
Join local cleanup efforts, food drives, or conservation projects. These opportunities
allow you to contribute to the community while meeting locals and fellow volunteers.

Support Local Businesses:

Frequent farmers' markets, cafes, or craft shops and strike up conversations with
vendors and patrons.

Attend local events like festivals, art shows, or concerts to immerse yourself in the
culture.

Explore Shared Spaces:

Libraries, coworking spaces, or community centers often host events or activities
where you can meet people.

3 Foster Community in Campsites

Campsites and boondocking spots are natural hubs for meeting other travelers.

Be Approachable:

Set up a friendly outdoor area with chairs or a table where others feel welcome to stop
by for a chat.

A simple greeting or compliment can start a conversation with a neighbor.

Host Shared Meals or Campfires:

Invite fellow travelers to share a meal, coffee, or an evening around the fire. It's an
easy way to bond and share stories.

Bring simple, shareable snacks or beverages to encourage group participation.

Organize Activities:

Suggest a group hike, yoga session, or stargazing night to connect with other campers.

4 Stay in Touch on the Road

Maintaining connections with those you meet enriches your van life network and
opens doors for future reunions.

Exchange Contact Information:
Swap phone numbers, social media handles, or email addresses with people you meet.
Use messaging apps like WhatsApp or Signal to stay in touch.

Create a Travel Network:
Start a group chat or online group with other van lifers to share location updates, tips,
or events.
Use shared maps or apps to coordinate meetups when your paths cross again.

Reconnect at Events:
Plan to attend van life gatherings or events where you know your new friends will be.

5 Find Groups Based on Shared Interests

Pursuing hobbies or interests on the road can help you meet like-minded individuals.

Outdoor Enthusiasts:
Join hiking, climbing, or kayaking groups to connect with others who share your
passion for the outdoors.

Creative Communities:
Attend art workshops, music events, or writing groups to find creative inspiration and
camaraderie.

Pet Owners:
If you travel with a pet, connect with other pet owners through dog parks, pet-friendly

events, or online groups.

6 Balance Solitude and Connection

While building community is rewarding, it's also important to balance social
interactions with the solitude that makes van life special.

Set Boundaries:
If you need downtime, communicate that politely to others and prioritize self-care.

Embrace Seasonal Connections:
Spend time building relationships when you're in social settings, then retreat into
nature for solitude when you need it.

Stay Selective:
Focus on building quality relationships rather than trying to meet everyone.

Real-World Example: Building Community on the Road

Mike and Jess, a couple traveling in their self-converted Sprinter, built a rich network
of friends and connections through intentional efforts:

- **Van Life Gatherings**: They attended Descend on Bend, where they met several couples and now plan future meetups together.
- **Local Volunteering**: While in Montana, they joined a park cleanup event and befriended locals who shared insider tips about the area.
- **Campsite Bonding**: At a remote desert boondocking spot, they organized a group hike and shared a potluck dinner with fellow travelers.
- **Staying Connected**: Mike and Jess started a private Instagram group with their new friends, sharing location updates and plan-

ning reunions.

Their approach allowed them to enjoy a balance of meaningful connections and the independence of van life.

Tips for Building Community on the Road
   Be Open and Approachable: Smile, greet others, and show genuine interest in their
   stories.
   Give Before You Take: Share advice, help with tasks, or contribute to group meals as a
   way to build goodwill.
   Use Technology to Your Advantage: Apps, social media, and forums make it easy to
   find and connect with others.
   Be Respectful of Space: While building connections is important, always be mindful of
   others' boundaries and privacy.

Building community on the road turns van life into more than just a journey—it creates a shared experience full of friendship, learning, and support. By connecting with fellow travelers, locals, and hobbyists, you'll enrich your adventures and find a sense of belonging wherever the road takes you.

6

Cooking on the Road

Cooking on the road doesn't have to be a chore. With the right setup, a little planning, and some creative thinking, you can enjoy delicious, satisfying meals that fit your lifestyle and energy needs. Whether you're a culinary enthusiast or a fan of simple, hearty meals, this chapter explores how to make cooking on the road easy, enjoyable, and efficient.

1. Stocking Your Mobile Pantry

A well-stocked pantry is the backbone of hassle-free cooking on the road. Whether you're boondocking far from grocery stores or whipping up a quick meal after a long day, having the right ingredients on hand ensures you're always prepared. Let's dive into how to build and organize a mobile pantry that balances long-lasting staples, fresh ingredients, and easy access.

1 Pantry Essentials for the Road

Start with non-perishable staples that form the foundation of versatile meals.

Dry Goods:
Grains and Pasta: Stock items like rice, quinoa, couscous, oats, and pasta for quick,
filling meals.
Legumes: Dried or canned beans, lentils, and chickpeas offer high-protein options for
soups, salads, and main dishes.
Flours and Baking Supplies: Include flour, sugar, baking powder, and yeast if you
enjoy baking or making fresh bread.
Canned Goods:
Choose items like tomatoes (diced, sauce, or paste), coconut milk, broth, and tuna for
versatile cooking.
Look for pop-top cans for convenience, especially if you don't want to rely on a can
opener.
Snacks and Quick Meals:
Keep granola bars, trail mix, dried fruits, and crackers for easy, on-the-go snacks.
Instant noodles or soup packets are great for emergencies or low-energy days.
Spices and Condiments:
A compact spice kit with basics like salt, pepper, garlic powder, paprika, cumin, and
chili flakes adds flavor to any meal.
Include condiments like olive oil, vinegar, soy sauce, mustard, and hot sauce. Store
these in small, refillable bottles to save space.

2 Fresh Ingredients for Versatility

Adding fresh ingredients to your pantry enhances meals and provides variety, even on
longer trips.

Produce That Lasts:
Choose hardy vegetables like potatoes, onions, carrots, and sweet potatoes, which can
last weeks without refrigeration.
Opt for fruits with a longer shelf life, such as apples, citrus, and unripe bananas.

Refrigerated Essentials:
Eggs: Packed with protein and versatile for breakfast, baking, or snacks.
Dairy: Store small quantities of cheese, butter, or yogurt for added flavor and
nutrients.
Greens: Spinach, kale, or mixed greens can last longer if stored in breathable produce
bags.

Perishable Additions:
Fresh herbs like cilantro or parsley add vibrant flavors; wrap them in damp paper
towels and store in a sealed bag to extend freshness.
Pre-cooked meats like chicken strips or deli turkey are convenient for quick meals.

3 Pantry Organization for Easy Access

A well organized pantry saves time and prevents frustration when cooking in a small
space.

Use Clear Storage Containers:
Store dry goods like rice, pasta, or flour in transparent, airtight

containers to keep
them fresh and visible.
Label containers with contents and expiration dates for easy identification.

Maximize Vertical Space:
Stackable bins or shelves can double your storage capacity. Use slim containers for
spices and canned goods to prevent clutter.

Categorize Your Pantry:
Group similar items together: grains and pasta, canned goods, snacks, and spices.
Dedicate specific areas for fresh produce, refrigerated items, and dry goods to avoid
rummaging.

Secure Your Pantry for Travel:
Use non-slip mats or bungee cords to keep containers and jars from sliding during
transit.
Magnetic strips or adhesive hooks can hold spice jars or small utensils securely on
walls.

4 Smart Shopping Tips for the Road

Efficient shopping keeps your pantry stocked without overloading your van.

Plan Ahead:
Create a weekly meal plan and shopping list based on your upcoming travel itinerary
and the availability of stores.
Prioritize ingredients with multiple uses, such as canned tomatoes for pasta sauces,

soups, and curries.

Shop Local:
Visit farmers' markets to stock up on fresh, local produce and specialty items.
Buying smaller quantities ensures fresher ingredients and minimizes waste.

Rotate Stock:
Use older items first to avoid spoilage. Adopt a "first in, first out" system for dry goods
and canned items.

Real-World Example: A Well-Stocked Pantry

Anna and Greg, full-time van lifers, have perfected their mobile pantry for flexibility
and efficiency:

- **Dry Goods**: Quinoa, pasta, and oats stored in clear, stackable containers.
- **Canned Goods**: Diced tomatoes, coconut milk, and black beans kept in a low-profile bin with dividers.
- **Snacks**: Trail mix and granola bars in an easily accessible drawer near the door for quick hikes.
- **Fresh Produce**: Sweet potatoes, apples, and a small bunch of bananas stored in a hanging fruit hammock.
- **Spices**: Magnetic spice tins mounted on the wall for their go-to flavors.
- **Refrigerated Essentials**: Eggs, cheese, and spinach stored in a 12V fridge with adjustable shelving.

Their organized system ensures they can quickly prepare meals without sifting through clutter, making van life cooking both efficient and enjoyable.

Tips for Stocking and Maintaining Your Pantry

Keep It Compact: Choose small or collapsible containers to save space and avoid
overstocking.

Think Multi-Purpose: Select ingredients that can be used in multiple meals to
maximize versatility.

Monitor Inventory: Regularly check your pantry and fridge for low-stock items and
expiration dates.

Invest in Quality Storage: Airtight containers and stackable bins can significantly
improve pantry organization and extend food freshness.

A well-stocked and organized mobile pantry is the foundation of stress-free cooking on the road. By focusing on durable staples, fresh ingredients, and efficient storage, you can create a system that ensures delicious, hassle-free meals wherever your adventures take you.

2. Essential Cooking Tools for the Road

Cooking in a van requires a balance of functionality, portability, and space-saving design. By selecting the right tools and equipment, you can prepare a wide variety of meals without feeling limited by your compact kitchen. This subsection dives into the must-have cooking tools for van life, ensuring that every meal is both enjoyable to make and easy to clean up.

1 Must-Have Cooking Equipment

Start with versatile, durable tools that form the backbone of your van kitchen.

Stove or Cooking Surface:

Propane Stoves: Dual-burner models like the Camp Chef Everest or Coleman Triton

are reliable, portable, and powerful enough for most meals.

Induction Cooktops: Ideal for vans with robust solar and battery setups, offering a

clean and flameless cooking option.

Portable Grills: Compact propane or charcoal grills are perfect for outdoor cooking and

grilling.

Pots and Pans:

Non-Stick Skillet: A high-quality, medium-sized skillet for frying, sautéing, and one

pan meals.

Medium Pot with Lid: Ideal for boiling pasta, making soups, or cooking grains.

Dutch Oven: Heavy-duty and multi-functional, perfect for baking, stews, and slow

cooking.

Utensils:

A spatula, ladle, tongs, and a wooden spoon are essentials for most recipes.

Choose silicone or heat-resistant materials for durability and easy cleaning.

Knife Set:

A chef's knife, paring knife, and serrated knife cover most kitchen tasks.

Store knives in a protective sheath or a magnetic strip to keep them secure.

Cutting Board:
Opt for a lightweight, compact board with non-slip edges.
Consider a dual-sided option to separate raw meat and vegetables.

2 Space-Saving and Multi-Functional Tools

When space is at a premium, choose tools that serve multiple purposes.

Collapsible Cookware:
Silicone strainers, mixing bowls, and colanders fold flat for easy storage.

Nesting Pots and Pans:
Look for sets that stack together neatly to save space.

Measuring Cups and Spoons:
Magnetic or nesting sets are compact and easy to store.

Sporks and Multi-Use Utensils:
Combine forks, spoons, and knives into one lightweight tool for simple meals.

3 Food Prep Essentials

Preparing ingredients efficiently is key to stress-free cooking in a small space.

Handheld Grater or Microplane:
Perfect for grating cheese, zesting citrus, or shredding small amounts of vegetables.

Peeler:
A compact, sharp vegetable peeler for quick prep.

Mixing Bowls:
Collapsible or nesting bowls for mixing, marinating, or serving.

Portable Blender:
A small USB-powered blender for smoothies, soups, or sauces.

4 Storage and Cleanup Tools

Keep your cooking tools organized and your space clean with these essentials.

Storage Solutions:

Use zippered pouches or small bins to group utensils, knives, and other tools.

Hang frequently used tools on magnetic strips or hooks to save counter space.

Cleaning Supplies:

Biodegradable dish soap and a sponge or scrubber for washing up. Microfiber towels for drying dishes and wiping down surfaces. A collapsible drying rack or mat for easy storage when not in use.

Trash and Recycling Bins:

Compact, lidded bins for trash, compost, and recycling to keep your kitchen tidy.

5 Outdoor Cooking Tools

Cooking outside can expand your options and reduce indoor mess.

Portable Grill or Fire Pit:

Perfect for grilling meats, vegetables, or even making s'mores.

Cast Iron Skillet:

Durable and ideal for cooking over open flames.

Campfire Tripod or Grate:

Allows for easy cooking over a campfire, especially in remote areas.

6 Optional Extras for Food Lovers

If you enjoy cooking more elaborate meals, consider these additional tools:

Immersion Blender:

Compact and versatile for pureeing soups, sauces, or making whipped cream.

Mandoline Slicer:
Great for preparing uniform slices of vegetables or fruit.

Thermometer:
A compact digital thermometer for precise cooking of meats or baked goods.

Real-World Example: A Compact Yet Functional Kitchen Setup
Luke and Emma, a couple traveling in their converted Sprinter van, keep their cooking
tools simple and effective:

- **Cooking Gear**: A dual-burner propane stove, a medium non-stick skillet, a nesting pot set, and a Dutch oven.
- **Utensils**: A silicone spatula, wooden spoon, tongs, and a multipurpose chef's knife.
- **Space-Saving Tools**: Collapsible silicone bowls and a grater stored in a drawer organizer.
- **Cleanup Supplies**: Biodegradable soap, a scrubber, and a roll-up drying rack.

Cost Breakdown:

- Stove: $120
- Cookware: $150
- Utensils and tools: $80
- Cleaning supplies: $30 **Total**: ~$380

Their setup allows them to prepare everything from simple one-pot meals to more elaborate dishes, all while keeping their kitchen tidy and manageable.

Tips for Choosing and Maintaining Your Cooking Tools
  Invest in Durability: Choose high-quality tools that can withstand frequent use and
  travel conditions.
  Prioritize Multi-Functionality: Select items that serve multiple purposes to save space
  and reduce clutter.
  Stay Organized: Use labeled bins, drawer dividers, or wall-mounted storage to keep
  tools accessible and secure.
  Keep It Clean: Rinse tools and cookware immediately after use to prevent messes from
  piling up.

By choosing essential, space-saving, and multi-functional cooking tools, you'll make meal prep on the road simple and enjoyable. With the right setup, you can cook like a pro, whether you're parked in a scenic forest or nestled in a cozy urban spot.

3. Meal Planning for Van Life

Meal planning is essential for van life. It saves time, reduces waste, and ensures you always have something nutritious and delicious to eat, no matter where you park. With thoughtful planning and a flexible approach, you can prepare meals that fit your energy needs, cooking setup, and available ingredients.

1 Why Meal Planning Matters on the Road
  Planning meals in advance brings multiple benefits for van life:

- **Efficiency**: Simplifies grocery shopping by focusing on ingredients you need for specific meals.
- **Waste Reduction**: Prevents spoilage of fresh produce and ensures leftovers are used creatively.
- **Cost Savings**: Avoids last-minute stops for expensive takeout or convenience store items.
- **Energy Conservation**: Reduces the need to improvise or cook elaborate meals after a long day.

2 How to Plan Your Meals

Successful meal planning starts with understanding your needs and preferences.

Assess Your Cooking Setup:

Consider the limitations of your stove, fridge, and pantry when choosing recipes.

Focus on meals that require minimal equipment and cleanup.

Plan for Flexibility:

Choose recipes that allow substitutions based on what's available. For example, swap

spinach for kale or rice for quinoa.

Include "assembly meals" like wraps or salads that require no cooking.

Think in Categories:

Breakfast: Quick and nutritious options like oatmeal, eggs, or smoothies.

Lunch: Easy-to-assemble meals such as sandwiches, wraps, or leftovers.

Dinner: Heartier meals like pasta, stir-fries, or one-pot soups.

3 Batch Cooking and Prepping

Cooking in bulk can save time and effort, especially when you're in remote locations or
on busy travel days.

Batch Cook Staples:
Cook large quantities of rice, quinoa, pasta, or beans, and store them in airtight
containers for easy reheating.

Prepare a big batch of soup, stew, or chili to divide into portions for future meals.

Pre-Chop Ingredients:
Wash and chop vegetables in advance for quick additions to stir-fries, salads, or
omelets.

Marinate proteins like chicken, tofu, or fish ahead of time to enhance flavor and save
cooking time.

Freeze Extras:
Freeze pre-cooked meals like curry, pasta sauce, or casseroles in portioned bags for
quick, hassle-free reheating.

4 Simplify Grocery Shopping

Meal planning makes grocery shopping more efficient and ensures you have
everything you need for your planned meals.

Make a List:
Write a list organized by sections: dry goods, fresh produce, dairy, and frozen items.

Use apps like AnyList or Google Keep to keep your shopping list accessible on the go.

Buy Multipurpose Ingredients:

Focus on items that work across multiple meals, like canned tomatoes, garlic, or eggs.

Choose long-lasting produce such as potatoes, onions, and apples.

Shop Local:
Visit farmers' markets for fresh, seasonal ingredients that can inspire new recipes.

5 Easy-to-Plan Meal Ideas

These meal ideas are simple to plan, versatile, and perfect for van life:

Breakfast:
Overnight oats with fruit and nuts.
Scrambled eggs with pre-chopped veggies.
Smoothies made with frozen fruit, yogurt, and protein powder.

Lunch:
Wraps with hummus, shredded carrots, and grilled chicken.
Cold pasta salad with olive oil, cherry tomatoes, and mozzarella.
Tuna or egg salad sandwiches with whole-grain bread.

Dinner:
One-pot pasta with garlic, spinach, and parmesan.
Stir-fried veggies with tofu and rice.
Grilled burgers or veggie patties with roasted potatoes.

6 Using Leftovers Creatively

Leftovers are a van life hero, reducing waste and creating easy meals.

Repurpose Ingredients:
Turn leftover roasted veggies into a breakfast hash or quesadilla filling.
Use extra rice or quinoa in fried rice, grain bowls, or soup.

Soup Base:
Combine leftover meats, veggies, and grains with broth for an easy,

hearty soup.

Freeze for Later:
If you can't finish leftovers immediately, freeze them in portioned containers for
future meals.

Real-World Example: Meal Planning on the Road
Jake and Maria, full-time van lifers, use meal planning to simplify their travel days
and maximize their cooking setup:

Weekly Planning:
They plan four main meals each week and rely on versatile staples like rice and canned
beans for flexibility.

Batch Cooking:
Jake prepares a large pot of chili on Sundays, dividing it into containers for easy
lunches and dinners.

Shopping Routine:
Maria shops once a week, focusing on fresh produce for the first half of the week and
relying on pantry staples later.

Leftover Strategy:
Leftover grilled chicken becomes taco filling, while extra veggies are used in omelets
or stir-fries.

Their system minimizes food waste and ensures they always have delicious meals,
even during busy travel days.

Tips for Meal Planning Success

Start Simple: Don't overcomplicate your plan—stick to recipes you know and enjoy.

Embrace Adaptability: Be ready to swap ingredients based on availability or cravings.

Prep in Advance: Chop veggies, cook grains, or marinate proteins ahead of time to
save effort later.

Keep Backup Meals: Stock quick, no-cook options like instant noodles or canned soup
for emergencies.

By planning your meals and preparing ahead, you'll make cooking on the road more efficient, enjoyable, and stress-free. Whether you're parked at a scenic overlook or in the middle of nowhere, meal planning ensures you can savor every bite of van life.

4. Easy Meal Ideas for the Road

Cooking on the road doesn't mean sacrificing flavor or variety. With a little creativity and the right ingredients, you can whip up quick, satisfying meals that suit your lifestyle and available tools. This section dives into easy, van-friendly meal ideas for breakfast, lunch, dinner, and even dessert—keeping you fueled and happy no matter where you are.

1 Breakfast: Start Your Day Right

A nourishing breakfast sets the tone for a productive day of travel or exploration.

Overnight Oats:
Mix rolled oats, milk (or plant-based alternatives), and a sweetener

like honey or
   maple syrup in a jar.
Add toppings like fresh fruit, nuts, or seeds in the morning for a portable, nutritious
   meal.
Breakfast Burritos:
Scramble eggs with sautéed onions, peppers, and shredded cheese.
Wrap in a tortilla and add hot sauce or salsa. Make extras to wrap in foil for reheating
   later.
Pancakes or Waffles:
Use a simple mix like Kodiak Cakes or make your own with flour, baking powder, milk,
   and eggs.
Top with fresh fruit, syrup, or nut butter. Cook on a portable griddle or skillet.
Yogurt Parfaits:
Layer yogurt with granola, berries, and a drizzle of honey for a quick, no-cook
   breakfast.

2 Lunch: Easy and Portable Meals
Midday meals should be quick to prepare and easy to eat on the go.
Wraps and Sandwiches:
Fill tortillas or sandwich bread with hummus, sliced veggies, deli meat, or leftover
   grilled chicken.
Add a handful of spinach or arugula for extra crunch and nutrition.
Cold Pasta Salad:
Combine cooked pasta with olive oil, cherry tomatoes, cucumbers, and mozzarella

cubes.

Add canned tuna or chickpeas for a protein boost.

Mason Jar Salads:

Layer dressing at the bottom of a jar, followed by sturdy vegetables (carrots,

cucumbers), protein (chicken, beans, or boiled eggs), and leafy greens on top. Shake

when ready to eat.

Quesadillas:

Spread shredded cheese, beans, and leftover veggies on a tortilla, fold in half, and

toast in a skillet.

3 Dinner: Hearty Meals for the End of the Day

Dinner is the perfect time to enjoy a warm, satisfying meal, especially after a long day.

One-Pot Pasta:

Combine pasta, diced tomatoes, garlic, spinach, and water in a pot. Simmer until the

pasta is cooked and the sauce thickens. Add parmesan for extra flavor.

Stir-Fried Rice or Noodles:

Use cooked rice or noodles, sauté with veggies, soy sauce, and scrambled eggs or tofu.

Add a dash of sesame oil for a rich flavor.

Tacos:

Fill corn or flour tortillas with ground beef, chicken, or beans, and top with shredded

lettuce, cheese, and salsa.

Chili:

Simmer canned beans, diced tomatoes, ground meat (optional), and chili spices in a pot. Serve with crackers or cornbread.

Grilled Meals:

Cook marinated chicken, fish, or veggie kebabs on a portable grill. Pair with roasted

potatoes or a simple salad.

4 Snacks and Sides

Keep these simple options on hand to round out meals or satisfy hunger between

stops.

Trail Mix:

Mix nuts, dried fruit, and chocolate chips for a quick energy boost.

Hummus and Veggies:

Pair store-bought or homemade hummus with carrots, celery, or bell pepper strips.

Cheese and Crackers:

Combine your favorite cheese with whole-grain crackers for a quick snack.

Hard-Boiled Eggs:

Prep a batch at the start of the week for protein-packed snacks.

5 Desserts: Sweet Treats on the Go

Don't forget to indulge your sweet tooth with these easy desserts.

S'mores:

Toast marshmallows over a campfire or portable burner, then sandwich between

graham crackers with chocolate.

Grilled Fruit:

Slice bananas, peaches, or pineapple, grill until caramelized, and serve with yogurt or

whipped cream.

No-Bake Energy Bites:
Combine oats, peanut butter, honey, and chocolate chips. Roll into bite-sized balls and
refrigerate for a sweet, healthy snack.

Real-World Example: A Day of Meals on the Road

Rachel, a solo van lifer, keeps her meals simple yet satisfying:

- **Breakfast**: Overnight oats with almond milk, topped with fresh blueberries and almonds.
- **Lunch**: A cold pasta salad with tuna, cherry tomatoes, and arugula, drizzled with olive oil.
- **Dinner**: A one-pot pasta dish with diced tomatoes, garlic, and spinach, topped with grated parmesan.
- **Snacks**: Trail mix and a few hard-boiled eggs kept in her fridge for quick energy.
- **Dessert**: Grilled pineapple slices with a sprinkle of cinnamon and a dollop of yogurt.

Her approach ensures minimal cleanup while offering variety and balanced nutrition.

Tips for Road-Friendly Meals

Prep Ingredients: Chop veggies, cook grains, and portion snacks at the start of the
week to simplify meal prep.

Prioritize One-Pot Meals: They save on cleanup and work well with limited cooking
equipment.

Use Versatile Ingredients: Eggs, beans, tortillas, and cheese can be used across multiple meals.

Keep It Flexible: Adapt meals to what you have on hand or what's available locally.

By focusing on easy, versatile meals, you'll keep cooking stress-free and enjoyable. Whether it's a quick wrap for lunch or a hearty chili for dinner, these ideas ensure that mealtime is one of the highlights of your van life adventure.

5. Cooking Outdoors vs. Indoors

Cooking in a van offers the flexibility to prepare meals either inside or outside, depending on your location, weather, and personal preferences. Both options come with their own set of advantages and challenges, but with the right setup, you can seamlessly transition between indoor and outdoor cooking to enjoy delicious meals wherever you are.

1 Benefits of Cooking Outdoors

Cooking outside allows you to embrace nature while keeping your van's interior fresh

and tidy.

Keeps Smells and Heat Out:

Cooking aromatic meals like fish or curry outdoors prevents lingering odors in your

van.

Heat from stoves or grills won't raise the temperature inside your living space.

Expands Your Workspace:

Outdoor cooking provides more space for prepping and setting up without feeling

cramped.
You can set up a portable table for chopping, grilling, or serving.

Enjoy Scenic Views:
Cooking outside immerses you in your surroundings, making mealtime more
enjoyable.

Great for Group Meals:
Outdoor cooking setups allow you to host and share meals with fellow travelers or
campsite neighbors.

2 Outdoor Cooking Equipment

To make outdoor cooking efficient and enjoyable, invest in the right tools.

Portable Stove or Grill:
Propane stoves like the Coleman Triton or a small camping grill work well for outdoor
use.
Consider a collapsible fire pit for grilling over an open flame.

Folding Tables and Chairs:
A sturdy, lightweight folding table provides ample prep and cooking space.
Add portable chairs for a comfortable outdoor dining setup.

Wind Protection:
Use a windscreen for your stove or grill to maintain consistent heat in breezy
conditions.

Outdoor Cooking Accessories:
A durable cutting board, lightweight cookware, and grilling utensils.
A camping lantern or headlamp for evening cooking.

3 Tips for Successful Outdoor Cooking

Scout Your Location:
Choose a flat, stable surface for setting up your stove or grill. Be mindful of fire restrictions in dry or high-risk areas.

Organize Your Tools:
Keep your utensils, spices, and cookware in a portable caddy for easy transport. Bring a collapsible sink or basin for quick cleanup.

Plan for the Elements:
Carry a tarp or canopy to cook comfortably in rain or intense sun. Use heavy-duty clips to secure lightweight items in windy conditions.

4 Benefits of Cooking Indoors

Indoor cooking is perfect for rainy days, urban camping, or when you're looking for convenience and privacy.

Weather-Proof and Convenient:
Cook comfortably in bad weather without worrying about wind, rain, or extreme temperatures.

Everything you need—ingredients, cookware, and utensils—is within reach.

More Secure and Private:
Cooking indoors allows you to prepare meals discreetly, especially in urban environments.

Controlled Environment:
Indoor setups provide better control over cooking conditions, such as wind-free burners and consistent lighting.

5 Indoor Cooking Setup

A well-designed indoor kitchen allows for efficient and safe meal prep.

Compact Stove:
Install a two-burner propane stove or a portable induction cooktop for flameless cooking.

Ventilation:
Use a roof vent fan or open windows to reduce steam, smoke, and odors.
A small battery-powered fan can improve airflow if you don't have a built-in vent.

Foldable Countertops:
Add a flip-up countertop extension to increase your prep space without compromising storage.

Fire Safety:
Keep a small fire extinguisher and a carbon monoxide detector in your van for safety.

6 Tips for Safe Indoor Cooking

Ventilate Well:
Always crack a window or use a fan when cooking with gas or propane indoors.

Choose Low-Odor Meals:
Focus on recipes with minimal lingering smells, like stir-fries or pasta dishes.

Keep Your Space Tidy:
Clean as you go to prevent grease buildup or spills from becoming hazards.

Real-World Example: Balancing Indoor and Outdoor Cooking

Nick and Laura, a couple traveling in their DIY-converted Ram ProMaster, seamlessly

switch between indoor and outdoor cooking based on their needs:

Outdoor Cooking Setup:

A dual-burner propane stove, foldable table, and camping grill make their outdoor

kitchen versatile.

They keep a set of collapsible silicone bowls and utensils in a portable bin for easy transport.

Indoor Cooking Setup:

A single-burner propane stove with a vent fan allows them to cook indoors during bad

weather.

They installed a small flip-up counter near the sink for extra prep space.

Meals:

Outdoor: Grilled salmon with roasted veggies over a campfire.

Indoor: One-pot pasta with tomato sauce and fresh basil.

Choosing the Right Option for Your Day

When deciding whether to cook indoors or outdoors, consider:

- **Weather**: Outdoor cooking is best in pleasant conditions, while indoor cooking shines during rain or wind.
- **Privacy**: In busy areas, indoor cooking offers more discretion.
- **Time and Effort**: Outdoor setups may require more time to prepare and clean, while indoor cooking is quicker.

Tips for a Smooth Transition Between Indoor and Outdoor Cooking

Stay Flexible: Be prepared to switch to indoor cooking if weather conditions change.
Keep Tools Accessible: Store cooking equipment in a way that's easy to grab for both indoor and outdoor use.
Adapt Recipes: Choose meals that can be prepared in either setting without major adjustments.

Cooking indoors and outdoors both have their unique benefits, and having the flexibility to enjoy both expands your options and enhances your van life experience. With the right tools and a little preparation, you can create delicious meals no matter where you decide to cook.

6. Save Time and Energy with Smart Cooking Hacks

Van life cooking doesn't need to be time-consuming or energy-intensive. With a few clever tricks and efficient habits, you can prepare delicious meals quickly while minimizing mess and resource usage. Whether you're working with limited power, water, or space, these hacks will streamline your kitchen routine and make life on the road even more enjoyable.

1 Optimize Ingredient Prep

Planning and prepping ingredients ahead of time can drastically reduce cooking effort.

Pre-Chop and Store:
Wash, peel, and chop vegetables in bulk at the start of the week. Store them in airtight
containers or zip-top bags for quick access.
Pre-slice fruits for snacks or toppings and store them in small reusable containers.

Use Ready-to-Go Ingredients:

Stock up on pre-washed greens, canned beans, and precooked grains like quinoa or
rice.

Keep a few jars of pre-made sauces or spice mixes to add flavor with minimal effort.

Batch Prep Proteins:

Cook larger quantities of chicken, tofu, or ground meat and store them in portions to
use in wraps, salads, or stir-fries throughout the week.

Hard-boil a batch of eggs to have a high-protein snack or meal ingredient ready.

2 Embrace One-Pot and One-Pan Meals

Minimize cleanup and simplify cooking with meals that require just one pot or pan.

One-Pot Meals:

Examples: Pasta with vegetables and sauce, chili, or soups.

Cook ingredients in stages in the same pot to layer flavors without creating extra
dishes.

One-Pan Wonders:

Roast a combination of proteins and vegetables on a single baking tray for an easy,
hands-off meal.

Use a large skillet for stir-fries, fried rice, or breakfast hashes.

Tips for Success:

Use non-stick or cast-iron cookware to reduce sticking and make cleanup faster.

Incorporate ingredients with similar cooking times to avoid over- or under-cooking.

3 Simplify Cleanup with Smart Tools

Streamlining cleanup saves time and preserves your water supply.

Use Foil and Parchment Paper:
Line baking trays or wrap food in foil for easy, no-mess cooking. Use parchment paper for oven meals to avoid baked-on residue.

Opt for Collapsible or Multi-Purpose Tools:
Use a collapsible dish tub for washing up or as a prep bin. A silicone spatula doubles as a stirring tool and scraper to remove stuck-on food before washing.

Clean As You Go:
Wash utensils and small items while larger dishes cook to avoid a pile-up.
Wipe down surfaces and stow ingredients immediately after use.

4 Leverage Time-Saving Appliances

Small, efficient appliances can reduce your cooking time and effort.

Pressure Cooker or Instant Pot:
Great for making soups, stews, and grains quickly with minimal hands-on time.

Immersion Blender:
Quickly blend soups, sauces, or smoothies directly in the pot without transferring to a blender.

Mini Food Processor:
Chop, shred, or mix ingredients like herbs, nuts, or dough in seconds.

5 Batch Cooking for Maximum Efficiency

Cooking larger portions at once can save time and energy.

Cook Once, Eat Multiple Times:
Make a large pot of soup, curry, or pasta sauce and portion it into

containers for later
   meals.
Freezer-Friendly Options:
Freeze extra portions in flat, stackable bags for easy reheating.
Mix and Match Ingredients:
Batch-cook staple ingredients like roasted vegetables or grains and combine them in
   different ways throughout the week to keep meals interesting.

6 Energy-Efficient Cooking Techniques
Conserving energy is crucial when cooking off-grid.
Lid It Up:
Always cook with a lid to trap heat and reduce cooking time.
Use Smaller Burners or Low Heat:
Match your pot size to the burner to avoid wasted heat.
Use a simmer setting whenever possible to save fuel.
Solar Cooking:
Invest in a portable solar oven for energy-free meal prep. Ideal for slow-cooking stews
   or baking in sunny climates.

7 Reduce Waste and Maximize Ingredients
Waste-free cooking helps you make the most of your resources.
Repurpose Leftovers:
Turn leftover roasted vegetables into a breakfast hash or quesadilla filling.
Use rice or quinoa from the previous night in fried rice or grain bowls.
Plan Around Perishables:
Use fresh ingredients early in the week and rely on pantry staples as your trip
   progresses.

Compost Scraps:
If you're in a suitable location, compost vegetable peels or coffee grounds instead of discarding them.

Real-World Example: Smart Cooking in Action
Sophie and Mark, full-time van lifers, have mastered the art of efficient cooking:

- **Prepping Ahead:** They batch-chop vegetables and marinate chicken at the start of each week.
- **One-Pot Dinners:** Their go-to meals include a hearty chili or pasta with spinach, garlic, and tomatoes.
- **Energy Conservation:** They use a solar oven to slow-cook stews while parked at sunny campsites.
- **Cleaning Hack:** Foil-lined baking trays make cleanup a breeze, and they wash dishes immediately after meals to save water.

Their streamlined process lets them enjoy flavorful meals with minimal time spent cooking or cleaning.

Tips for Smart Cooking Success
Plan Ahead: Prep ingredients in advance to simplify meal prep.
Choose Multi-Purpose Tools: Select tools that can handle multiple tasks to save space
and time.
Clean as You Go: Stay on top of cleanup to reduce post-meal stress.
Batch Cook Smartly: Cook in larger portions to have meals ready for busy or off-grid
days.

By adopting these time-saving and energy-efficient cooking hacks, you'll spend less time stressing over meals and more time enjoying the freedom of van life. From batch cooking to creative cleanup strategies, these tips ensure that your kitchen routine is simple, efficient, and satisfying.

7. Real-World Example: Cooking on the Road

Cooking on the road varies depending on your setup, habits, and the environments you travel through. To bring the tips and tools together, let's take a closer look at how a real van-living couple, **Megan and Josh**, have mastered their mobile kitchen. Their approach balances simplicity, creativity, and practicality, ensuring delicious meals with minimal stress, no matter where they park.

1 Daily Routine and Meal Prep

Megan and Josh's daily cooking routine is designed for efficiency and enjoyment:

Morning Prep:

Breakfast is a quick, no-fuss meal, such as overnight oats or scrambled eggs with

leftover veggies.

They use this time to boil water for coffee, which they store in a thermal carafe to stay

warm for hours.

Any fresh produce that needs chopping for the day's meals is prepped in the morning

to save time later.

Midday Meals:

Lunch is often a cold pasta salad, wraps, or leftovers from the previous night's dinner.

Megan preps salads in mason jars during their grocery shopping day, layering the
dressing at the bottom to keep the greens crisp.

Dinner Focus:
Dinner is the most elaborate meal of the day, often cooked outdoors when the weather
permits.
They favor one-pot meals, such as stir-fries or stews, paired with fresh bread or rice
cooked in their portable rice cooker.

2 Kitchen Setup

Their van kitchen is compact but thoughtfully organized:

Cooking Equipment:
A dual-burner propane stove for both indoor and outdoor cooking.
A cast-iron skillet for versatile cooking, from searing meat to baking cornbread.
A collapsible silicone pot and nesting pans for space-saving storage.

Refrigeration:
A 45L 12V fridge that holds perishables like dairy, vegetables, and proteins.
Megan maximizes fridge space by using stackable containers and vacuum-sealing
items like marinated chicken or leftovers.

Storage:
Josh built a pantry cabinet with pull-out bins for easy access to canned goods, grains,
and spices.
A hanging fruit hammock keeps bananas, apples, and citrus within reach and free of
bruises.

Cleaning Essentials:

A collapsible sink and biodegradable soap keep dishwashing manageable.

Microfiber towels double as dish dryers and cleaning cloths.

3 Typical Weekly Meal Plan

Megan and Josh rely on a flexible but structured meal plan that ensures variety
without complicating their routine:

Breakfasts:

Day 1: Overnight oats with chia seeds, blueberries, and almond milk.

Day 2: Breakfast burritos with scrambled eggs, salsa, and shredded cheese.

Day 3: Pancakes with maple syrup and a side of fresh orange slices.

Lunches:

Day 1: Wraps filled with hummus, spinach, grilled chicken, and shredded carrots.

Day 2: Cold pasta salad with cherry tomatoes, cucumbers, and feta cheese.

Day 3: Tuna and egg salad sandwiches on whole-grain bread.

Dinners:

Day 1: One-pot chili with black beans, ground turkey, and diced tomatoes.

Day 2: Grilled salmon and asparagus with roasted sweet potatoes.

Day 3: Stir-fried veggies and tofu served over jasmine rice.

4 Their Approach to Meal Planning

Megan and Josh follow a few simple principles to keep meals enjoyable and
manageable:

Batch Cooking and Multi-Use Ingredients:

They prepare a large batch of grains (rice or quinoa) at the start of the week, which can
be repurposed for stir-fries, salads, or as a dinner side.
Protein like chicken is grilled in bulk, then used in wraps, salads, and as a dinner main.
Flexibility:
They adapt meals based on what's in their pantry or available at local markets.
If they're short on time, a can of soup or instant noodles paired with fresh greens
becomes a quick, satisfying option.
Specialty Nights:
Once a week, they create a "themed night" like taco Tuesday or pasta night to keep
things exciting.

5 Weather-Based Cooking Decisions
Cooking decisions often depend on the day's conditions:
Outdoor Cooking:
On sunny, mild days, they set up their portable grill and foldable table to enjoy meals
al fresco.
Grilled options include marinated chicken skewers, veggie burgers, or foil-packet
meals with potatoes and seasoned veggies.
Indoor Cooking:
When it's rainy or windy, they cook inside the van, focusing on meals that produce
minimal steam or odors, like pasta with a simple tomato sauce or quick stir-fries.

6 Challenges and Solutions

Like any van lifers, Megan and Josh face occasional cooking challenges:

Limited Water Supply:

To conserve water, they use pre-soaked grains and avoid recipes that require excessive

rinsing or boiling.

They clean utensils immediately after use to reduce the need for extensive washing

later.

Space Constraints:

They keep prep simple by using a single cutting board and consolidating all their

ingredients before starting.

Dishes are stacked and washed in the order they were used, from cleanest to dirtiest.

7 Cost and Setup Breakdown

Their kitchen setup and cooking habits have been designed with cost-efficiency in

mind:

Kitchen Equipment:

Dual-burner propane stove: $120

Cast-iron skillet: $30

12V fridge: $900

Collapsible cookware and utensils: $75

Total: ~$1,125

Weekly Food Budget:

They spend an average of $75–$100 per week, shopping at a mix of grocery stores and

farmers' markets.

8 Takeaways from Megan and Josh's Experience

Stay Organized: A well-planned kitchen setup saves time and reduces stress during
   meal prep.

Cook in Batches: Preparing staples like grains and proteins ahead ensures easy,
   versatile meals throughout the week.

Adapt to Conditions: Flexibility in choosing indoor vs. outdoor cooking keeps
   mealtime enjoyable.

Use Multi-Functional Tools: Simplifying your kitchen gear makes it easier to
   transition between meal types and setups.

Cooking on the road doesn't have to be complicated. By following Megan and Josh's example, you can create a mobile kitchen that's practical, efficient, and a joy to use—whether you're preparing gourmet meals or quick, comforting favorites.

8. Tips for Success

Mastering the art of cooking on the road requires more than just the right tools and
   recipes—it's about creating habits and strategies that make meal prep efficient,
   enjoyable, and stress-free. These tips build on the principles of van life cooking to
   ensure you're always ready to whip up something delicious, no matter the challenges.

1 Plan, But Stay Flexible

Having a plan is important, but van life often brings unexpected changes.

Meal Planning Basics:

Create a weekly meal plan that balances fresh ingredients early in the week with

pantry staples for later.

Include meals that use overlapping ingredients to minimize waste and maximize

variety.

Adaptability:

Be ready to swap recipes based on what's available locally or what you have left in your

pantry.

Keep a mental (or written) list of "go-to meals" that you can assemble quickly with

staples like beans, rice, pasta, or eggs.

2 Organize Your Kitchen Space

A tidy and efficient kitchen setup is key to stress-free cooking.

Declutter Regularly:

Remove unused or unnecessary tools and gadgets to make space for essentials.

Keep food items organized by type (e.g., spices, grains, snacks) and store frequently

used items in easy-to-reach spots.

Label Everything:

Label containers, jars, and bins to quickly identify contents without opening

everything.

Use clear storage for dry goods to monitor quantities at a glance.

Secure Items for Travel:
Use non-slip mats, bungee cords, or magnetic strips to keep items from moving while
driving.

3 Simplify Cleanup

Efficient cleanup keeps your van feeling fresh and avoids wasted water.

Minimize Dishes:
Use one-pot or one-pan recipes to reduce the number of items that need washing.
Eat directly from the cookware or use reusable bowls and utensils to cut down on
dishware.

Clean as You Cook:
Wash utensils and wipe down surfaces while meals simmer or bake.
Use a microfiber towel to dry dishes immediately and avoid clutter.

Prevent Messes:
Line baking trays with foil or parchment paper for easy cleaning.
Scrape plates and cookware into a trash bag or compost bin before washing to keep
your sink clear.

4 Make the Most of Your Ingredients

Van life cooking thrives on creativity and resourcefulness.

Use Ingredients Fully:
Save vegetable scraps for homemade broth or composting.
Repurpose leftovers into new meals—roast veggies can become a hash, and leftover
rice can transform into fried rice or grain bowls.

Shop Smart:

Prioritize versatile ingredients like eggs, beans, and tortillas that can be used across

multiple meals.

Stock up on shelf-stable items during sales or when you're near a grocery store.

5 Stay Safe While Cooking

Safety should always be a priority in your mobile kitchen.

Fire Safety:

Keep a small fire extinguisher and fire blanket accessible in case of emergencies.

Never leave a stove or grill unattended while cooking.

Ventilation:

Always open windows or run a roof vent fan when cooking indoors to prevent carbon

monoxide buildup.

Use a portable fan if natural ventilation isn't sufficient.

Proper Storage:

Store perishable items in a 12V fridge or cooler with ice packs.

Check expiration dates regularly and discard spoiled items promptly.

6 Save Time with Batch Cooking and Prep

Preparing ingredients and meals in advance makes daily cooking faster and easier.

Batch Cooking Tips:

Cook large quantities of grains, beans, or proteins at the start of the week to use in

multiple meals.

Portion out meals into stackable containers for easy reheating.

Pre-Chopped Ingredients:

Chop and store vegetables in resealable bags or containers for quick

access during busy
days.
Marinate proteins like chicken or tofu ahead of time for extra flavor and convenience.

7 Experiment with New Recipes

Cooking on the road is an opportunity to explore new flavors and techniques.

Incorporate Local Ingredients:
Shop at farmers' markets or roadside stands to try fresh, regional produce.
Incorporate local spices or specialty items into your meals for variety.

Adjust Recipes for Simplicity:
Modify complex recipes to suit your van kitchen by reducing the number of steps or
ingredients.
Focus on meals that require minimal prep and equipment.

8 Stay Powered Up

Managing energy use is critical, especially when cooking off-grid.

Energy-Saving Techniques:
Cook with lids on pots and pans to retain heat and reduce cooking time.
Use a thermal cooker or solar oven for slow-cooking meals without constant energy
use.

Backup Options:
Keep non-cook options like canned soup, instant noodles, or sandwich ingredients for
low-energy days.

Real-World Example: Tips from a Full-Time Van Lifer

Lila, a solo traveler in her converted Sprinter van, has developed a system to make
cooking on the road seamless:

- **Meal Planning**: She plans three days ahead, balancing fresh produce with shelf-stable items.
- **Smart Tools**: Lila uses a single cast-iron skillet and a compact rice cooker for most meals, reducing the need for multiple pots and pans.
- **Batch Cooking**: She makes large portions of chili or pasta sauce and freezes them in flat bags for easy storage and quick reheating.
- **Outdoor and Indoor Balance**: On sunny days, she grills vegetables and proteins outdoors; in bad weather, she switches to her portable propane stove inside.
- **Efficiency Hacks**: Lila lines her baking trays with foil to minimize cleanup and uses a collapsible sink to conserve water.

Top Tips for Success

Keep It Simple: Focus on recipes that require minimal steps and ingredients.

Stay Flexible: Adapt your meals to available ingredients, weather, and your energy
levels.

Organize Thoughtfully: A tidy kitchen setup makes cooking more enjoyable and
efficient.

Prioritize Safety: Ventilate properly, store perishables correctly, and have safety tools
on hand.

Embrace Creativity: Experiment with new recipes, ingredients, and

techniques to keep
  meals exciting.

With these practical tips, you can elevate your van life cooking experience. Whether you're whipping up a quick breakfast or hosting a cozy outdoor dinner, these strategies will help you create delicious meals while saving time, energy, and resources.

7

Planning Your First Adventure

You've built your van, stocked your pantry, and mastered the art of cooking on the road. Now it's time to hit the open road for your first adventure! Planning your inaugural journey can feel both exciting and daunting, but with a little preparation, you can ensure a smooth and enjoyable experience. This chapter breaks down the key factors to consider when mapping out your first van life trip, from choosing your destination to budgeting, safety, and flexibility.

1. Choosing Your First Destination

Choosing the right destination for your first van life adventure sets the tone for your journey. It's important to strike a balance between excitement and practicality, ensuring you feel confident and prepared while exploring a location that inspires you. This section dives into the key considerations and tips to help you pick the perfect spot for your first outing.

1 Start Close to Home

For your first trip, it's a good idea to stay relatively close to home.

Test Your Setup:

A shorter trip allows you to test your van systems, cooking setup, and sleeping

arrangements without committing to a long journey.

If any issues arise—like a leaky faucet or an uncomfortable bed—you can address

them easily before tackling a more ambitious route.

Safety Net:

Being near home or familiar locations provides peace of mind in case you forget

something essential or encounter a challenge.

Suggested Destinations:

Nearby national or state parks.

Scenic campgrounds within a 2–3 hour drive.

Local beaches, forests, or quiet rural areas.

2 Consider Accessibility and Comfort

Beginner-friendly destinations help ease you into van life.

Good Road Conditions:

Choose locations with paved or well-maintained roads, especially if your van isn't

built for rugged terrain.

Avoid routes with steep grades or tight switchbacks unless you're experienced with

your vehicle.

Campsite Amenities:

Look for campgrounds with basic amenities like restrooms, water, and electricity

hookups. These can make your first trip more comfortable while reducing the stress of managing all your van's systems.

If you're feeling adventurous, try dispersed camping areas with clear maps and

reviews for safe parking spots.

Urban vs. Nature:

Decide if you'd prefer to stay near urban conveniences like grocery stores and gas

stations or immerse yourself in remote, natural settings.

3 Choose a Destination That Excites You

Your first adventure should inspire excitement and curiosity.

Bucket List Ideas:

Visit a place you've always wanted to explore but haven't yet. This could be a nearby

lake, a mountain range, or a famous landmark.

Incorporate activities you enjoy, such as hiking, kayaking, or photography, to make

the trip memorable.

Seasonal Considerations:

Research seasonal weather patterns and plan accordingly. For instance, choose a cool

mountain destination in summer or a warmer coastal spot in winter.

Be aware of peak tourist seasons, as crowded locations might detract from your

experience.

Scenic Routes:

Choose destinations with scenic drives to enhance the journey itself. Roads that wind

through forests, along coastlines, or past rolling hills can be as rewarding as the

destination.

4 Balance Challenges with Confidence

While it's important to step out of your comfort zone, don't overwhelm yourself on
your first trip.

Start with Easier Logistics:
Avoid destinations that require complex permits, remote navigation, or high-risk
conditions.
Gradually build your skills and confidence before tackling rugged or off-grid locations.

Stay Connected:
Opt for destinations with reliable cell service or easy access to help if needed. Apps like
Campendium and iOverlander can provide information about coverage in various
areas.

Real-World Example: A First Destination Done Right

Sarah and Jake, first-time van lifers, chose a scenic state park 150 miles from home for
their inaugural trip.

Why It Worked:
The park offered well-maintained campsites with electricity, water hookups, and
restroom facilities, easing their transition to van life.
Activities included easy hiking trails and a small lake where they could paddle board.
The drive included a stretch of scenic highway, making the journey as enjoyable as the
destination.

Outcome:

They learned how to manage their van systems in a low-pressure environment and

left feeling confident to explore farther on their next adventure.

Tips for Choosing Your First Destination

Stay Close: Choose a location within a day's drive to reduce travel stress and allow

time to focus on your setup.

Pick Beginner-Friendly Locations: Prioritize accessible routes and campgrounds with

basic amenities for added comfort.

Incorporate Interests: Select a destination that aligns with your hobbies, whether it's

hiking, photography, or simply relaxing by the water.

Research Thoroughly: Use apps, maps, and online reviews to ensure your destination

meets your expectations and is safe for overnight parking.

Plan for Seasonal Comfort: Avoid extreme weather by choosing the right destination

for the time of year.

Your first destination doesn't have to be far or extravagant—it just needs to be somewhere that excites you while providing a manageable introduction to van life. By selecting a location that balances adventure with comfort, you'll set yourself up for a successful and enjoyable first outing.

2. Mapping Your Route

Mapping your route is a vital part of planning your first van life adventure. A well-thought-out route not only ensures you reach your destination smoothly but also allows you to make the most of your journey. With the right tools and strategies, you can enjoy scenic drives, convenient stops, and a flexible itinerary that enhances your overall experience.

1 Plan for Comfort and Convenience

Your first adventure should prioritize ease and enjoyment over complexity.

Choose Manageable Drive Times:

Aim to drive no more than 4–6 hours a day. This leaves time for rest, meals, and

exploration.

Factor in potential delays, such as traffic or roadwork, and give yourself buffer time to

avoid feeling rushed.

Incorporate Scenic Stops:

Research points of interest along your route, such as parks, viewpoints, or quirky

roadside attractions.

Apps like **Roadtrippers** can help identify interesting places to break up the drive.

Locate Rest Stops:

Use resources like **iOverlander**, **FreeRoam**, or **Google Maps** to find rest areas, truck

stops, or gas stations where you can park and stretch.

Plan for bathroom breaks and snack stops to stay comfortable on the road.

2 Select the Right Tools for Navigation

Reliable navigation tools are essential for van life.

Digital Maps:

Apps like **Google Maps** or **Waze** offer real-time traffic updates and route adjustments.

Gaia GPS or **AllTrails** can be helpful if your route includes remote or off-grid

destinations.

Offline Maps:

Download offline maps for areas with poor cell coverage to ensure you can still

navigate.

Apps like **Maps.me** or **Google Maps Offline** let you save maps for use without an

internet connection.

Paper Maps:

Carry a physical map or road atlas as a backup, especially for areas with unreliable

connectivity.

3 Plan Strategic Stops Along the Way

Break up long drives with well-timed stops to recharge and explore.

Rest Areas and Overnights:

Identify safe, overnight parking spots if your route spans multiple days. These could

include Walmart parking lots, truck stops, or free camping areas.

Apps like **Park4Night** can help find safe and legal spots to rest.

Dining and Refueling:

Look for gas stations and grocery stores along the way to refuel your van and restock

supplies.

Plan meals that align with stops to save time and energy.
Activities and Attractions:
Include short hikes, museums, or scenic viewpoints to add variety and excitement to
your journey.

4 Stay Flexible with Your Itinerary

While planning is essential, maintaining flexibility allows you to adapt to unexpected
changes.
Monitor Conditions:
Check weather forecasts and road conditions before and during your trip. Adjust your
route if severe weather or closures are expected.
Websites like **511.org** provide real-time road updates.
Build in Buffer Time:
Allow extra time for detours, unexpected delays, or impromptu stops at interesting
locations.
Avoid scheduling your days too tightly to keep the trip enjoyable and stress-free.
Be Prepared to Adjust:
If a campsite or stop doesn't meet your expectations, have a backup plan or alternative
destination in mind.

5 Focus on Fuel Efficiency and Costs

Careful route planning can help minimize fuel costs and maximize your travel budget.
Optimize Your Route:
Plan routes that avoid excessive backtracking or unnecessary detours.

Highways and main roads often offer better fuel efficiency compared to winding or
hilly backroads.

Track Gas Stations:

Use apps like **GasBuddy** to find the cheapest fuel prices along your route.

Plan refueling stops in areas where gas prices are lower.

Real-World Example: A Well-Mapped Route

Anna and Brian, first-time van lifers, planned their route to a national park 300 miles
from home:

Route Plan:

Their route included a mix of highways and scenic byways, with stops at a rest area
and a small town for lunch.

They downloaded offline maps using Google Maps in case they lost cell service near
the park.

Stops Along the Way:

Rest Stop 1: A clean, well-reviewed area with picnic tables for a quick breakfast.

Attraction: A roadside waterfall marked on their Roadtrippers app.

Gas Stop: A station in a small town with low fuel prices and a nearby grocery store for
supplies.

Flexibility:

When unexpected rain delayed their hike at the park, they adjusted their plan to
explore a nearby museum instead.

Outcome:

Their careful route planning ensured a smooth, enjoyable trip with minimal stress and
no surprises.

Tips for Mapping Your Route
Start with Major Stops: Identify your destination and key waypoints, then fill in
details like rest areas and attractions.
Plan for Breaks: Schedule regular stops to avoid fatigue and make the journey more
enjoyable.
Keep Navigation Tools Handy: Use a mix of digital apps, offline maps, and paper
backups to stay on track.
Stay Flexible: Be ready to adjust your route or schedule to adapt to road conditions or
unexpected opportunities.
Track Costs: Monitor fuel prices and refueling stops to keep your budget in check.

Mapping your route is about more than getting from point A to point B—it's an opportunity to make the journey as memorable as the destination. With careful planning and the right tools, you can enjoy a smooth, scenic, and stress-free ride every step of the way.

3. Budgeting for Your Trip

A well-planned budget ensures you can enjoy your first van life adventure without financial stress. By anticipating costs and making informed choices, you can stretch your dollars while still enjoying everything the road has to offer. This section breaks down key expenses, money-saving tips, and strategies to create a flexible yet practical budget for your trip.

1 Estimate Your Major Expenses

Start by identifying the core expenses for your trip.

Fuel Costs:

Calculate the total miles of your trip and divide by your van's average miles per gallon

(MPG) to estimate fuel consumption.

Use apps like **GasBuddy** to find fuel prices along your route for a more accurate cost

estimate.

Example:

Trip distance: 500 miles round trip.

MPG: 15 miles per gallon.

Fuel cost: $4 per gallon.

Total fuel cost: 500 ÷ 15 × $4 = ~$133.

Camping Fees:

Research the cost of campgrounds or RV parks. Prices vary, from $10–$30 per night

for basic sites to $50+ for those with full hookups.

Look for free camping options, such as dispersed camping on BLM land or sites listed

on apps like **iOverlander** or **Campendium**.

Food and Supplies:

Break down your food budget into groceries and dining out.

For a weeklong trip, plan ~$40–$70 per person for groceries, depending on how much

you eat and cook.

Factor in additional supplies like propane, water, or toiletries.

Entertainment and Activities:
Include entry fees for parks, museums, or other attractions.
Plan for rentals (e.g., kayaks, bikes) or tours you might want to enjoy.
Emergency Funds:
Set aside at least 10–15% of your total budget for unexpected costs, such as van
repairs, medical needs, or last-minute campsite fees.

2 Track Variable Costs

Some costs depend on your travel habits and choices.

Driving Style and Routes:
Driving at steady speeds and avoiding aggressive acceleration can improve fuel
efficiency.
Opt for direct routes when possible to save on fuel.

Dining Choices:
Limit eating out to occasional treats and focus on cooking in your van.
Pack snacks to avoid impulse purchases at gas stations.

Campsite Amenities:
Choose campgrounds based on your needs. Basic sites are cheaper but may lack water
or electricity.
Save money by boondocking (free camping) where possible, but ensure you have the
necessary supplies for off-grid stays.

3 Money-Saving Tips

Keep costs low without sacrificing your experience.

Fuel Efficiency:
Inflate tires to the correct pressure and keep your van well-

maintained to improve fuel
economy.

Drive at moderate speeds; vans often perform best around 55–65 mph for fuel
efficiency.

Free and Low-Cost Camping:

Use apps like **FreeRoam** to find free camping spots.

Consider Walmart parking lots or truck stops for overnight stays on travel days (check
local regulations).

Groceries Over Dining Out:

Plan meals ahead of time and stick to your grocery list to avoid overspending.

Buy in bulk for non-perishable items like rice, pasta, or canned goods.

Use Passes and Discounts:

If visiting multiple national parks, purchase an **America the Beautiful Pass** ($80
annually) for unlimited entry.

Look for discounts at campgrounds, such as senior or military rates.

4 Budgeting Tools and Strategies

Keep your spending on track with these tools:

Apps and Spreadsheets:

Use apps like **Trail Wallet, Mint,** or a simple Google Sheets spreadsheet to track your
expenses.

Break your budget into categories like fuel, camping, food, and activities for better
organization.

Set a Daily Budget:

Allocate a specific amount for daily expenses, such as $50/day for

fuel, food, and
camping. Adjust as needed based on actual costs.

Cash vs. Card:
Carry a small amount of cash for places that don't accept cards, but use a credit card
for larger purchases to track spending more easily.

Real-World Example: A Budget-Friendly Trip

Tina, a solo van lifer, planned a 4-day trip to a national park 300 miles away:

Fuel Costs:
Round trip: 600 miles ÷ 18 MPG × $3.75/gallon = ~$125.

Camping Fees:
3 nights at $20/night = $60.

Food:
Groceries: $50 for snacks, meals, and drinks.
Dining out: One meal at a local café, ~$15.

Activities:
National park entry fee: $30 (single-vehicle fee).

Total Budget: $125 + $60 + $50 + $15 + $30 = **$280**

Tina saved money by packing her own food and choosing a basic campsite with no
hookups, leaving her with extra funds for unexpected expenses or souvenirs.

Tips for Staying on Budget

Plan Ahead: Research all major costs, including fuel, camping, and attractions, before
your trip.

Track Spending: Monitor expenses daily to ensure you stay within your budget.

Be Flexible: Adjust plans if unexpected costs arise, such as opting for free camping or a
cheaper activity.

Set Priorities: Spend on what matters most to you—whether it's splurging on a great
meal or saving for a bucket-list experience.

Avoid Overpacking: Extra weight in your van reduces fuel efficiency, so pack only what
you need.

Budgeting for your first van life adventure doesn't mean sacrificing fun—it's about making intentional choices that align with your goals and resources. With a solid plan and smart money-saving strategies, you'll be free to focus on the joys of the journey, not the stress of expenses.

4. Packing for Success

Packing for your first van life adventure requires thoughtful planning to balance preparedness with efficiency. Overpacking can clutter your van, while underpacking might leave you without essentials. This section helps you create a comprehensive packing plan to ensure your trip is smooth, comfortable, and enjoyable.

1 Create a Packing Checklist

A detailed checklist keeps you organized and prevents forgotten items.

Categories to Include:

- **Clothing**: Weather-appropriate layers and footwear.

- **Kitchen Supplies**: Cooking tools, utensils, and pantry staples.
- **Personal Items**: Toiletries, medications, and travel documents.
- **Emergency Gear**: First-aid kit, flashlight, and multi-tool.
- **Van Essentials**: Spare tire, jumper cables, and fluids.
- **Tip**: Organize your checklist by van zones (e.g., bedroom, kitchen, storage) to streamline packing.

2 Pack for the Weather

Be prepared for changing weather conditions by packing versatile clothing and gear.

Clothing Layers:

Base layer: Moisture-wicking shirts and leggings.

Mid-layer: Sweatshirts, sweaters, or fleece jackets for insulation.

Outer layer: Waterproof jackets and pants for rain protection.

Footwear:

Comfortable shoes for driving and walking.

Hiking boots if your trip involves outdoor exploration.

Sandals or slip-ons for campsite use.

Seasonal Accessories:

Hats, gloves, and thermal socks for cold weather.

Sun hats, sunglasses, and sunscreen for hot climates.

3 Essentials for Your Van's Systems

Your van's functionality depends on having the right tools and maintenance supplies.

Vehicle Maintenance:

Spare tire, jack, and tire repair kit.

Basic tools like a wrench, screwdriver set, and duct tape.

Fluids: Engine oil, coolant, and windshield washer fluid.

Power and Water:

Extra propane tanks or fuel canisters.
Extension cords and adapters for shore power hookups.
Water hose and filter for refilling your tank.
Cleaning Supplies:
Broom and dustpan for quick cleanups.
Multi-purpose cleaner and microfiber cloths for surfaces.
Trash bags and a small recycling bin.

4 Kitchen and Cooking Supplies

A functional kitchen setup ensures you can prepare meals with ease.
Cookware and Utensils:
Pots, pans, and a cutting board.
Multi-use utensils like a spatula, tongs, and a chef's knife.
Collapsible bowls and strainers to save space.
Pantry Staples:
Non-perishables like pasta, rice, beans, and canned goods.
Cooking essentials: Salt, pepper, oil, and your favorite spices.
Refrigeration and Storage:
Stackable containers for leftovers.
A hanging fruit hammock or produce bags for fresh items.
Coffee and Tea Setup:
Portable French press or pour-over cone for coffee lovers.
A small kettle or pot for boiling water.

5 Sleeping Comfortably

A good night's sleep is crucial for a successful trip.
Bedding:
A comfortable mattress or sleeping pad.
Warm blankets and sleeping bags for cooler nights.
Lightweight sheets and pillows for warmer climates.
Blackout Curtains or Covers:

Ensure privacy and block out light for better sleep.
Comfort Accessories:
Earplugs and an eye mask for noisy or bright campsites.
A portable fan or heater for temperature control.

6 Emergency and Safety Supplies

Be prepared for unexpected situations with the right safety gear.
First-Aid Kit:
Include bandages, antiseptic wipes, pain relievers, and any personal medications.
Add extras like a thermometer, tweezers, and a space blanket.
Navigation Tools:
Physical maps or an atlas as a backup to GPS devices.
Compass for outdoor adventures.
Lighting and Communication:
A rechargeable flashlight or headlamp.
Solar or battery-powered lanterns for the campsite.
A power bank or portable charger for devices.
Emergency Contacts:
Keep a printed list of important numbers, including roadside assistance, medical
services, and family.

7 Personal Items and Comforts

Don't forget the small touches that make van life feel like home.
Toiletries:
Travel-sized shampoo, soap, toothbrush, and toothpaste.
Quick-dry towels and biodegradable wipes for convenience.
Entertainment:
Books, e-readers, or a deck of cards for downtime.
A portable speaker or headphones for music and podcasts.

Personal Touches:
Photos, small decorations, or souvenirs to personalize your space.

Real-World Example: Packing for a Weekend Adventure
Liam and Sophie, first-time van lifers, planned a 3-day trip to a nearby national park.
Essentials Packed:
Clothing: 3 outfits each, rain jackets, and hiking boots.
Kitchen: A skillet, pot, French press, and a cooler for perishables.
Bedding: A lightweight sleeping bag and an extra blanket for chilly nights.
Safety Gear: First-aid kit, headlamp, and a multi-tool.
Challenges Faced:
They forgot a portable table for outdoor cooking but improvised with a flat rock at the
campsite.
Lesson learned: Double-check the checklist before leaving!
Outcome:
Despite the hiccup, their thoughtful packing allowed them to enjoy comfortable meals,
great hikes, and cozy nights under the stars.

Tips for Packing Like a Pro
Start with a Checklist: Cover all categories to ensure nothing is left behind.
Pack Versatile Items: Focus on multi-functional tools and clothing to save space.
Test Your Gear: Try out cooking tools, bedding, and other essentials before your trip.
Stay Organized: Use labeled bins or packing cubes to separate items for easy access.

Review and Adjust: After each trip, refine your packing list based on what you used and what you didn't.

Packing for success is all about preparation and balance. By focusing on essentials, staying organized, and prioritizing comfort, you'll be ready to tackle your first van life adventure with confidence.

5. Prioritize Safety and Security

Safety and security are foundational to a successful van life adventure. While van travel is inherently exciting, ensuring your well-being and protecting your belongings should always be a top priority. This section provides practical advice on how to stay safe, secure, and prepared for the unexpected.

1 Research and Plan Ahead

Careful preparation can help you avoid risky situations and make informed choices.

Campsite Research:

Use apps like **Campendium, iOverlander,** or **Park4Night** to find safe and well-reviewed
campsites.

Look for areas with amenities such as lighting, water access, and nearby facilities.

Avoid isolated spots if you're traveling solo or new to van life.

Local Knowledge:

Research crime rates and safety tips for the regions you plan to visit.

Check local laws regarding overnight parking or camping to avoid fines or conflicts.

Emergency Contacts:

Compile a list of local emergency numbers, including police, medical services, and
roadside assistance.

Share your travel itinerary with a trusted friend or family member.

2 Protect Your Van and Belongings

Keeping your van secure ensures peace of mind while on the road.

Lock and Secure:

Always lock your doors and close windows when leaving the van, even briefly.

Install deadbolts, window locks, or security bars for added protection.

Alarms and Trackers:

Consider a car alarm system or motion-sensor lights to deter theft.

Use a GPS tracker to locate your van if it's stolen.

Conceal Valuables:

Store cash, electronics, and passports out of sight in a hidden compartment or
lockbox.

Avoid leaving valuables on display, even when parked in seemingly safe areas.

3 Be Mindful of Personal Safety

Take precautions to keep yourself safe in unfamiliar environments.

Trust Your Instincts:

If a location feels unsafe, trust your gut and move to a different spot.

Park near other campers or in well-lit areas to reduce isolation.

Set Boundaries:

Politely but firmly decline interactions with strangers if you feel uncomfortable.

Carry a personal alarm, whistle, or pepper spray for added protection.

Stay Connected:

Keep your phone charged and ensure you have cell service or a satellite communicator
for remote areas.

Share your location with a trusted friend through apps like **Google Maps** or **Life360**.

4 Prepare for Emergencies

Being ready for unexpected situations can save time and stress.

First-Aid Kit:

Include bandages, antiseptics, medications, and tools like tweezers and scissors.

Familiarize yourself with basic first-aid procedures for common injuries.

Vehicle Safety:

Carry a spare tire, jack, and tire repair kit.

Keep jumper cables, a portable battery pack, and extra fluids (oil, coolant, etc.) in your
van.

Know how to access and use your van's toolkit.

Weather Preparedness:

Check weather forecasts daily and plan accordingly.

Carry emergency supplies like a thermal blanket, rain gear, and extra food and water.

5 Navigate Safely

Smart navigation practices can reduce risks on the road.

Avoid Driving at Night:

Stick to daytime driving when visibility is better, and wildlife is less active.

Plan Rest Stops:

Schedule regular breaks to avoid fatigue and ensure you're alert behind the wheel.
Follow Road Conditions:
Check for closures, construction, or hazards using apps like **511.org** or local
government websites.

Real-World Example: Staying Safe on the Road
Emma, a solo van lifer, incorporates safety measures into her daily routine:

- **Campsite Choice**: She uses **Campendium** to find well-reviewed, well-lit campsites and avoids parking in isolated areas.
- **Van Security**: Emma installed a deadbolt on her van door and hides valuables in a lockbox under her bed.
- **Emergency Preparedness**: She carries a first-aid kit, a fire extinguisher, and a spare tire kit.
- **Personal Safety**: Emma keeps pepper spray in an easily accessible spot and uses a personal alarm when hiking alone.

Outcome: Emma's proactive approach allows her to feel secure and confident while exploring remote and urban areas alike.

Tips for Prioritizing Safety and Security
Park Smart: Choose well-lit, populated areas and avoid parking near sketchy or
unregulated spaces.
Secure Your Van: Lock all doors and windows, and invest in additional security
features like alarms or trackers.
Stay Alert: Be aware of your surroundings, especially in unfamiliar

locations.

Keep Emergency Supplies Handy: A well-stocked first-aid kit and vehicle repair tools
are non-negotiable.

Trust Your Instincts: If something doesn't feel right, don't hesitate to change
locations or seek assistance.

By prioritizing safety and security, you can enjoy your first van life adventure with confidence and peace of mind. With the right precautions and preparedness, you'll be ready to handle challenges and focus on the freedom and joy of life on the road.

6. Embrace Flexibility and Fun

No matter how meticulously you plan, your first van life adventure will have its surprises. Embracing flexibility and focusing on fun will help you navigate the unexpected and make your journey more memorable. This subsection explores strategies to adapt to changes, maximize enjoyment, and create a mindset that transforms challenges into opportunities.

1 Plan, but Stay Open to Change

Having a plan is essential, but rigidity can detract from the joys of the road.

Leave Room for Spontaneity:

Avoid scheduling every minute of your day. Instead, allow for unplanned stops, scenic
detours, or relaxing downtime.
If you see a roadside farm stand, quirky museum, or inviting trail,

give yourself the
freedom to explore.

Prepare for the Unexpected:

Weather, traffic, or campsite availability might force changes to your itinerary. Have
backup plans or alternative routes ready.

Use apps like **Campendium** or **iOverlander** to find last-minute campsites or parking
options.

Adapt to Your Energy Levels:

If you feel fatigued or overwhelmed, don't hesitate to adjust your plans for a slower
pace. Van life is about freedom, not pressure.

2 Celebrate the Small Moments

Focusing on the journey, not just the destination, helps you savor the unique
experiences of van life.

Appreciate the Views:

Take a few minutes to enjoy sunrise at a roadside rest stop or sunset from your
campsite.

Snap photos or jot down notes in a travel journal to remember the highlights.

Enjoy Local Experiences:

Stop at a small-town café or farmer's market to connect with the local culture.

Chat with other travelers or locals—you might get great tips or new perspectives.

Pause and Recharge:

Schedule time to simply relax in your van, read a book, or nap in a

hammock. Balance
activity with rest for a more fulfilling adventure.

3 Turn Challenges into Opportunities

Not everything will go as planned, but adopting a positive mindset can transform
setbacks into stories.

Weather Changes:
Rain ruining your hiking plans? Explore a nearby town, museum, or indoor café
instead.
Too hot to cook inside? Switch to a refreshing no-cook meal and enjoy it outside.

Unexpected Detours:
Road closures or delays might introduce you to hidden gems you hadn't considered
visiting.
Use the extra time to explore a roadside attraction or scenic viewpoint.

Minor Mishaps:
Forgot an item? Treat it as an opportunity to simplify or learn how to adapt creatively.

4 Find Joy in the Simplicity of Van Life

Van life is about embracing a minimalist lifestyle that prioritizes experiences over
possessions.

Simplify Your Day:
Appreciate the ease of preparing a simple meal or the joy of sleeping under the stars.
Focus on the freedom of being untethered from the constraints of everyday life.

Celebrate Small Wins:

Managed to park in the perfect spot for sunset? Found the ideal cup of coffee at a

roadside café? Relish these moments.

Celebrate progress, like mastering a new aspect of van maintenance or discovering an

efficient packing system.

Real-World Example: Finding Fun in Flexibility

Lauren and Matt, new to van life, planned a trip to a coastal national park. Midway

through their journey, unexpected rain washed out their beach day plans:

Adaptation:

Instead of sulking, they pivoted to exploring a nearby seaside town, where they

discovered a charming bookstore and a fantastic seafood restaurant.

In the evening, they parked at a scenic overlook, played board games, and listened to

the rain on the roof—a new favorite van life memory.

Takeaway:

Their ability to embrace flexibility and enjoy each moment made the trip a success,

even though it didn't follow their original plan.

Tips for Embracing Flexibility and Fun

Go with the Flow: Allow yourself to deviate from your itinerary to pursue unexpected

opportunities.

Prioritize Joy: Focus on experiences that make you happy, whether that's a

spontaneous hike or a leisurely coffee break.
Stay Positive: View challenges as part of the adventure rather than setbacks.

Be Open to New Connections: Meeting other travelers or locals can lead to new

friendships and valuable advice.

Document Your Journey: Capture the highs and lows in photos or a journal to reflect

on later—these moments often become the best stories.

By embracing flexibility and fun, you'll unlock the full potential of your first van life adventure. Challenges will become learning experiences, and unplanned moments might turn into the highlights of your trip. With an open mind and a sense of curiosity, you'll create memories that last a lifetime.

7. Real-World Example: A First Adventure Success Story

Let's look at how a real-life first van life adventure unfolded to highlight the importance of preparation, flexibility, and embracing the unexpected. **Jake and Mia**, a couple new to van life, embarked on a 4-day road trip to explore a nearby national park. Their experience shows how thoughtful planning combined with a willingness to adapt can turn a simple trip into an unforgettable journey.

1 The Initial Plan
Destination:
Jake and Mia chose a popular national park 200 miles from home, known for its

stunning trails and scenic campsites.

Route:

Their planned route included a mix of highways and scenic byways, with a halfway

stop at a rest area to refuel and stretch.

They used Google Maps to outline their route and downloaded offline maps to ensure

navigation in areas without cell service.

Campsites:

They reserved a campsite with water and electrical hookups for their first night, easing

into van life with some creature comforts.

For the second night, they planned to boondock on public land using coordinates

found on Campendium.

2 What Went Right

Thoughtful Preparation:

Their packing checklist ensured they had all essentials, from kitchen tools to

emergency supplies.

Mia prepped meals in advance, including marinated chicken for grilling and a big

batch of pasta salad.

Scenic Stops Along the Way:

On the drive to the park, they detoured to a roadside farm stand where they picked up

fresh peaches and honey.

A stop at a small-town coffee shop turned into an impromptu exploration of a local art

gallery.

Efficient Campsite Setup:
Their organized van layout allowed for quick setup at the first campsite. They spent
their first evening enjoying grilled chicken and watching the sunset.

3 The Unexpected Challenges

Weather Changes:
On the second day, unexpected rain turned their planned hike into a muddy mess.
Rather than pushing through, they opted to visit a nearby visitor center and learned
about the park's history.

Navigation Issues:
While driving to their boondocking site, they encountered a road closure. Using their
offline maps, they rerouted to a different public land area, arriving just before sunset.

Minor Equipment Failures:
Their portable fridge stopped working briefly due to a loose connection. Fortunately,
Jake's multi-tool allowed him to fix the issue, highlighting the importance of packing
tools.

4 Highlights of the Trip

Memorable Campfire Evening:
At the boondocking site, they built a small campfire and roasted marshmallows under
a clear night sky filled with stars.
This unplanned moment became the most cherished memory of the trip.

Improvised Fun:
When rain disrupted outdoor plans, they played card games inside the van, paired with
a pot of hot tea. The cozy atmosphere turned an obstacle into an opportunity to relax.

Wildlife Encounter:
On the final day, an early morning drive through the park rewarded them with a
sighting of deer grazing near the road, a reminder of nature's beauty.

5 Key Takeaways

Jake and Mia learned valuable lessons that set them up for future adventures:

Planning Pays Off:
Their organized packing and meal prep saved time and reduced stress.

Flexibility is Key:
Being willing to adjust their itinerary turned challenges into unexpected joys.

Connection with Nature:
Slowing down to appreciate small moments, like stargazing or wildlife encounters,
made the trip unforgettable.

6 Budget Breakdown

Jake and Mia's total expenses for their 4-day adventure were well within their $500
budget:

- Fuel: $85
- Campsites: $40 (1 night with hookups, 1 free boondocking night)
- Food: $70 (groceries)

- Entry Fees: $30 (park pass)
- Miscellaneous: $25 (farm stand purchases and coffee shop treats)

Total: $250

They saved money by cooking their own meals, choosing a mix of paid and free
campsites, and limiting unnecessary expenses.

7 Lessons for First-Time Adventurers

Be Over-Prepared: Thoughtful packing and pre-trip checks ensure you're ready for
anything.

Adapt to Challenges: Embrace detours, weather changes, or equipment hiccups as part
of the journey.

Savor the Journey: Small, unplanned moments—like a farm stand visit or card game
often become the most memorable.

Stay Budget-Conscious: Combining free activities, efficient driving, and home
cooked meals keeps costs low without sacrificing fun.

8 Why Their First Adventure Was a Success

Jake and Mia's first van life trip succeeded because they combined careful planning
with an open-minded attitude. They embraced the unexpected, stayed flexible, and
focused on enjoying the experience rather than achieving perfection.
Their story
illustrates that the heart of van life isn't about flawless execution but about the

freedom to explore, adapt, and create lasting memories.

By following their example, you can approach your first adventure with confidence
and excitement, ready to make the most of whatever the road has in store.

8. Tips for Your First Adventure

Your first van life adventure is an exciting milestone, and a little preparation goes a long way toward making it successful. These tips will help you navigate the challenges, embrace the joys, and make the most of your journey.

1 Start with Manageable Goals
Choose a Nearby Destination:
Aim for a location within a day's drive to minimize the stress of long-distance travel.
Pick a destination with beginner-friendly amenities like well-maintained
campgrounds or public facilities.
Focus on Simplicity:
Don't overcomplicate your itinerary. A few planned stops or activities leave room for
flexibility and spontaneity.
Test Your Setup:
Treat your first trip as a trial run to learn how your van systems work, what you've
packed correctly, and what might need adjustment.

2 Double-Check Essentials Before Departure

Van Systems:
Test your water, power, and heating systems to ensure they're functioning properly.

Check tires, brakes, fluids, and battery health to avoid mechanical issues.

Packing:
Use a checklist to confirm you've packed essentials like a first-aid kit, kitchen tools,
bedding, and clothing for all weather conditions.

Emergency Prep:
Ensure your roadside assistance membership is active and carry emergency contacts.

Familiarize yourself with the locations of nearby repair shops, gas stations, and
hospitals.

3 Plan Your Route, But Stay Flexible

Prioritize Comfort:
Opt for routes with well-maintained roads and avoid areas with heavy traffic or
difficult terrain if you're new to driving a van.

Schedule Breaks:
Plan rest stops every 2–3 hours to stretch, eat, or explore roadside attractions.

Have Backups:
Use apps like **iOverlander** and **Campendium** to save alternate campsites and stops in
case your first choice isn't available.

4 Budget Wisely
Estimate Costs:

Plan for fuel, food, camping fees, and activities. Add an extra 10–15% for unexpected
  expenses.
Save on costs by cooking meals in your van, using free campsites, and limiting
  unnecessary purchases.
Track Spending:
Use apps like **Trail Wallet** or a simple spreadsheet to monitor your expenses during the
  trip.
Emergency Fund:
Set aside cash or accessible savings for unexpected repairs or changes in plans.

5 Focus on Safety and Security
Choose Safe Parking:
Park in well-lit, populated areas and avoid isolated spots if traveling solo.
Use trusted apps to find verified campsites and rest areas.
Stay Alert:
Lock your van whenever you leave it, and keep valuables hidden.
Carry personal safety tools like a flashlight, whistle, or pepper spray.
Prepare for Emergencies:
Pack a fully stocked first-aid kit, spare tire kit, and multi-tool.
Ensure you have enough food and water to last 2–3 days longer than your planned trip
  in case of delays.

6 Embrace Flexibility and Enjoy the Journey
Be Open to Changes:
If weather or other circumstances disrupt your plans, pivot to alter-

native activities or destinations.

Treat setbacks as opportunities to explore something new or enjoy downtime in your van.

Slow Down:
Van life isn't about rushing from point A to B. Take time to savor scenic views, relax, and immerse yourself in the experience.

Document Your Trip:
Capture photos, write journal entries, or record videos to remember the highlights of your first adventure.

7 Learn and Adjust for the Future

Take Notes:
Keep a list of what worked and what didn't, from packing to route choices.

Write down any items you wish you had brought or things you didn't use.

Refine Your Setup:
After your trip, reorganize your van based on how you used the space and tools during your journey.

Celebrate Small Wins:
Every trip teaches you something new. Celebrate your successes, whether it's cooking your first van meal or navigating a challenging road.

Real-World Example: First Adventure Tips in Action

Chris and Megan, a couple planning their first trip, used these tips to ensure their success:

- **Goal**: A 3-day trip to a state park 150 miles away.
- **Preparation**: They double-checked their van systems, tested their propane stove, and packed essential tools like a tire repair kit and flashlight.
- **Flexibility**: When their first campsite was unexpectedly closed, they used Campendium to find a nearby alternative and turned the detour into an opportunity to explore a charming local town.
- **Safety**: They parked near other campers, locked their van whenever they left, and kept their phone charged for emergencies.

Outcome: By embracing the unexpected and focusing on the journey, Chris and Megan enjoyed a stress-free trip filled with scenic views, delicious meals, and newfound confidence for future adventures.

Quick Checklist for First-Timers

Plan Your Destination: Choose a nearby, accessible location with beginner-friendly amenities.

Test Your Setup: Ensure your van systems, tools, and supplies are ready to go.

Pack Smart: Use a checklist to cover essentials without overpacking.

Stay Flexible: Be ready to adapt your plans to changing conditions or new opportunities.

Prioritize Safety: Lock your van, research campsites, and carry emergency supplies.

Have Fun: Focus on the experiences, big or small, that make the journey memorable.

Your first van life adventure is an opportunity to learn, explore, and enjoy the freedom of the road. By following these tips, you'll set yourself up for a successful trip that leaves you excited and ready for the next one.

8

Money-Saving Hacks

Van life offers freedom and adventure, but it doesn't have to break the bank. With some clever hacks and intentional choices, you can cut costs without sacrificing the joy of the journey. This chapter dives into practical strategies to save money on fuel, food, camping, and more, so you can stretch your budget and make the most of life on the road.

1. Fuel-Saving Strategies

Fuel is often one of the biggest expenses for van lifers, but smart practices can reduce
costs.

Drive Efficiently:
Maintain a steady speed and avoid rapid acceleration or braking to maximize fuel
efficiency.
Stick to highways or well-paved roads whenever possible, as off-roading or steep
climbs burn more fuel.

Plan Your Routes:
Use apps like **GasBuddy** to find the cheapest fuel stops along your

route.

Combine errands and activities to minimize unnecessary driving.

Lighten Your Load:

Overloading your van increases fuel consumption. Pack only what you need and

remove excess weight regularly.

Maintain Your Van:

Regular maintenance, such as keeping tires inflated to the correct pressure and

changing oil on schedule, ensures optimal performance and fuel efficiency.

2. Save on Camping Costs

Camping fees can add up quickly, but there are plenty of ways to stay overnight

without spending a fortune.

Boondocking:

Take advantage of free camping opportunities on public lands like BLM land or

national forests. Apps like **iOverlander** or **Campendium** can help you find safe, legal

spots.

Memberships and Discounts:

Invest in camping memberships like **Passport America**, which offers discounts at

participating RV parks.

Many parks and campgrounds offer senior, military, or group discounts—be sure to

ask.

Urban Overnight Parking:

Use free overnight parking options like Walmart, Cracker Barrel, or

truck stops (where
permitted). Always check local regulations to avoid fines.
Stay Longer:
Some campgrounds offer discounts for extended stays, which can be cost-effective if
you plan to stay in one area for a while.

3. Frugal Food and Cooking Tips

Eating well on the road doesn't have to be expensive.
Cook Your Own Meals:
Avoid dining out by preparing meals in your van. Stick to simple, versatile recipes that
use affordable staples like rice, beans, and pasta.
Batch-cook meals like soups or stews and store leftovers for quick reheating.
Shop Smart:
Shop at discount grocery stores, farmers' markets, or co-ops for fresh, affordable
produce.
Buy in bulk when possible to save on staples like grains, oats, and canned goods.
Minimize Food Waste:
Plan meals to use up perishable ingredients before they spoil.
Store leftovers in airtight containers and invest in a small freezer for long-term
storage.
Use Free Resources:
Take advantage of free condiments, utensils, and napkins from gas stations or diners
(within reason).

4. Budget-Friendly Entertainment

Adventure and fun don't have to cost a fortune.

Explore Free Attractions:

Many national parks, beaches, and trails offer free or low-cost entry. Use passes like **America the Beautiful** for unlimited access to federal lands.

Seek out free local events like festivals, farmers' markets, or art shows in the towns
you visit.

Enjoy the Outdoors:

Hiking, swimming, stargazing, or simply relaxing in nature are free ways to enjoy van
life.

Invest in affordable outdoor gear like hammocks or portable chairs to enhance your
experience.

Borrow Instead of Buying:

Check out books, audiobooks, or DVDs from local libraries, many of which offer free
membership to travelers.

Use free apps like **AllTrails** to find nearby hikes or **Audible** for entertainment while
driving.

5. Save on Utilities and Supplies

Managing utilities wisely helps you save on essentials like water and electricity.

Water Conservation:

Fill your water tanks at free public faucets, truck stops, or campgrounds instead of
buying bottled water.

Use biodegradable soap to safely wash dishes or shower outdoors when permitted.

Solar Power:

Invest in solar panels to reduce reliance on paid hookups for electricity.

Use energy-efficient appliances and rechargeable devices to save on power.

DIY Cleaning Supplies:

Make your own cleaning solutions using vinegar, baking soda, and essential oils for a

cheaper and eco-friendly alternative.

Repurpose Items:

Use reusable containers, bags, and utensils to minimize waste and avoid buying

single-use items.

6. Work and Travel

Earning while traveling can supplement your budget and allow you to explore for

longer.

Remote Work:

Take advantage of remote work opportunities, such as freelance writing, graphic

design, or teaching online. Websites like **Upwork** and **Fiverr** offer platforms to find

gigs.

Many van lifers use Wi-Fi hotspots or public libraries for internet access.

Seasonal Jobs:

Consider seasonal work like fruit picking, park ranger positions, or event staff roles.

Websites like **CoolWorks** list short-term opportunities perfect for travelers.

Sell Your Skills:
Offer services like photography, van builds, or social media management to other
travelers or locals.
Create and sell handcrafted goods at local markets or online.

7. DIY Repairs and Upgrades

Learning basic van maintenance and repair skills can save you money and time.

Learn the Basics:
Watch online tutorials or attend workshops to learn how to change tires, replace
filters, or fix minor electrical issues.
Carry a well-stocked tool kit for on-the-road repairs.

Preventive Maintenance:
Regularly inspect your van for wear and tear to catch issues early and avoid costly
repairs.

Secondhand Solutions:
Buy used parts or materials from thrift stores, scrap yards, or online marketplaces like
eBay or Craigslist.

8. Real-World Example: Money-Saving Success

Ben and Rachel, a couple traveling full-time in their converted van, save an average of
$500 per month using these strategies:

- **Fuel**: They drive at steady speeds and plan efficient routes, cutting

their fuel expenses by 20%.
- **Camping**: 70% of their nights are spent boondocking, with occasional stays at low-cost campgrounds for showers and amenities.
- **Food**: They cook almost all their meals in the van, spending about $60 per week on groceries.
- **Repairs**: Ben learned basic maintenance skills, saving hundreds by doing his own oil changes and minor repairs.

9. Quick Money-Saving Hacks

Use Free Apps: Find free camping, cheap fuel, and local events.
DIY Everything: From cooking to repairs, doing it yourself saves big.
Buy in Bulk: Stock up on non-perishables to reduce grocery trips.
Limit Driving: Stay in one area longer to save on fuel.
Maximize Memberships: Use discount cards and passes to cut costs.

Van life doesn't have to drain your bank account. With these money-saving hacks, you can travel further, explore longer, and focus on what truly matters: the freedom and adventure of the open road.

9

Conclusion

Van life is more than a mode of travel—it's a lifestyle that offers freedom, adventure, and the chance to reconnect with what truly matters. As you embark on this journey, you'll discover that the road has as much to teach you as any destination. By thoughtfully preparing your van, planning your trips, and embracing the inevitable surprises, you'll turn your dream of life on the road into a reality.

Throughout this book, we've explored the essential elements of van life, starting with choosing the right van to suit your needs and equipping it for self-sufficiency. We've tackled the balance between comfort and practicality, learned how to create a cozy and functional home on wheels, and mastered cooking delicious meals in a compact space. With chapters on planning adventures and saving money, you now have a toolbox of hacks to navigate the challenges and joys of life on the move.

But van life is about more than hacks and logistics—it's about mindset. Flexibility, creativity, and a sense of curiosity are your greatest assets. Whether you're troubleshooting a mechanical issue, adjusting plans due to weather, or finding joy in the simplicity of a quiet morning in the wilderness, van life encourages you to embrace the unexpected and grow from the experience.

As you take to the road, remember that every journey is unique. The van life community is diverse and full of stories, advice, and inspiration, so lean into the connections you make along the way. Celebrate the highs, learn from the lows, and always keep your sense of adventure alive.

If this guide has been helpful for you, we'd be very appreciative if you could take a few minutes to leave a review on Amazon. Your feedback not only helps us improve but also guides fellow travelers on their new adventures.

The open road is calling. Your van is ready. The only thing left to do is start. Here's to your journey—wherever it may lead. Safe travels!

10

References

This book draws on a mix of practical advice, industry knowledge, and contributions from van life enthusiasts to provide a comprehensive guide. Below is a list of references that inspired and supported the ideas shared throughout the book:

Van Life Community Resources
    Campendium (https://www.campendium.com) – Comprehensive database for
      campgrounds, reviews, and boondocking sites.
    iOverlander (https://www.ioverlander.com) – Crowdsourced app for finding free
      camping, water fill stations, and more.
    FreeRoam (https://www.freeroam.app) – Camping app with overlays for BLM lands,
      cell coverage, and road conditions.
    Park4Night (https://www.park4night.com) – Resource for finding urban parking
      spots and scenic stopovers.

Vehicle and Maintenance Guidance

GasBuddy (https://www.gasbuddy.com) – App for locating affordable fuel options.

Van Maintenance Blogs and Forums: Insights from communities such as Reddit's

r/VanLife and Expedition Portal.

YouTube Tutorials: Channels like Kombi Life, Eamon and Bec, and Far Out Ride for DIY

van builds and maintenance tips.

Cooking and Pantry Organization

Minimalist Baker (https://minimalistbaker.com) – Simple, travel-friendly recipes.

Camping Recipe Blogs: Inspiration from websites like Fresh Off the Grid and The

Adventure Bite for outdoor and compact cooking.

Budget and Financial Planning

Passport America (https://www.passportamerica.com) – Discount camping

membership program.

National Park Service (https://www.nps.gov) – Information on the America the

Beautiful Pass for park access.

Outdoor Adventures and Route Planning

Roadtrippers (https://www.roadtrippers.com) – Trip planning tool for finding scenic

routes and attractions.

AllTrails (https://www.alltrails.com) – Hiking and outdoor activity resource.

Gaia GPS (https://www.gaiagps.com) – Navigation tool for off-grid adventures.

Inspiration and Lifestyle Insights
Books:
The Art of Van Life by Foster Huntington – Inspiration and insights into van life
culture.
How to Live in a Van and Travel by Mike Hudson – A practical guide to van life.
Blogs and Podcasts:
The Van Life Podcast – Personal stories and tips from the van life community.
Go-Van (https://www.go-van.com) – Blog with tips, lifestyle articles, and van life
stories.

Miscellaneous Tips
CoolWorks (https://www.coolworks.com) – Platform for finding seasonal jobs to
support van travel.
Google Maps & Offline Maps – Essential tools for navigation and planning remote
routes.

Personal Experiences and Contributions
Stories from van lifers in online communities like Facebook groups and forums.
Anecdotal insights from van life YouTubers, travel bloggers, and Instagram accounts.

This curated list highlights the resources, tools, and inspiration that shaped the guidance provided in this book. By diving deeper into these references, you'll find even more tips, ideas, and support to enrich your van life experience.

Made in the USA
Middletown, DE
13 July 2025